Forces of Our Time

Forces of Our Time

The Dynamics of Light and Darkness

by

Hooper C. Dunbar

George Ronald
Oxford

George Ronald, *Publisher*
Oxford
www.grbooks.com

© Hooper C. Dunbar 2009
All Rights Reserved

Reprinted 2010

A catalogue record for this book is available
from the British Library

ISBN 978-0-85398-538-9

Cover design: Steiner Graphics

Printed by Cromwell Press Group

Contents

Ours is a supremely pivotal time.
The gathering of great energies across the planet is clear to see,
but few have any real notion of their origin or ultimate effect.
May these pages help in understanding
what is actually taking place
and why.

Preface

As *Forces of Our Time* arrives at publication, I am honoured to write about the work from the perspective of those who had the privilege of assisting Mr Dunbar.

Most of us first experienced *Forces of Our Time* as students in Mr Dunbar's class. In those days, in the late 1980s, gatherings of Bahá'í World Centre staff took place in a building called 'the hall', a simple upstairs room with folding chairs in a spot that is now one of the lower Terraces on Mount Carmel. At a weekly evening study class 50 or 60 of us gathered with a sense of excitement and anticipation: we had no idea where the class would go but we knew it would be thrilling.

Our class was the fruit of Mr Dunbar's personal study of the Bahá'í Revelation. He had become aware, especially as he studied the writings of 'Abdu'l-Bahá and Shoghi Effendi, of a recurring pattern of statements that explained the development of reality, first as spirit, which was then shaped by intention into structures. Wanting to investigate this, he had gathered all the published writings of 'Abdu'l-Bahá and Shoghi Effendi (this was before the days of databases of the sacred writings), copied out all the relevant quotations and arranged them by date. He first taught a class on this material at Louhelen Bahá'í School in Davison, Michigan in the early 1980s. When Mr Dunbar taught the same material in his Monday night study class at the Bahá'í World Centre, a number of volunteers audio-taped and transcribed the class sessions, with the intention that the transcriptions could form the basis of a book.

As I was leaving the World Centre in June 1989, full of trepidation, Mr Dunbar and I had a conversation about turning transcripts of talks into books and he suggested that I take the

Forces transcripts with me and see what I could do with them. The opportunity to participate in the project was a parting gift to me from Mr Dunbar: I took the spiritual intoxication of his class, in the form of hundreds of pages of transcripts, with me into my unknown new life.

The transition of *Forces* from transcripts of Mr Dunbar's words spoken at Louhelen and at his evening class in Haifa into the form of a book was primarily a work of rearrangement. In classes focused on particular passages from Shoghi Effendi's writings, Mr Dunbar had spoken about a particular theme on many different occasions. I gathered together all the parts of the transcripts that addressed each core idea, arranged them and added some topic sentences for paragraphs and sections. The book is therefore, to a large extent, Mr Dunbar's spoken words rearranged: it has the direct, straightforward quality of spoken language because that is what it was. Coming as it does out of Mr Dunbar's classes at the World Centre and Louhelen, it is addressed to an audience with a basic familiarity with Bahá'í scriptures and institutions.

Mr Dunbar's heavy responsibilities as a member of the Universal House of Justice kept the manuscript buried for more than 15 years but the sense that this material is becoming ever more relevant prompted him to bring it out of the depths of saved computer files and complete the project. The descriptions of Bahá'í institutions were brought into conformity with their current state of development, some material was added and some stylistic changes were made.

Mr Dunbar requested that I express his thanks to the many collaborators who have helped with the project over the years. The contributions made in compiling quotations, making transcriptions of hours of talks, reviewing recordings and offering assistance with editing helped bring the project to fruition. On behalf of the helpers, I feel impelled to respond that we ourselves are the ones who are grateful.

Holly Hanson

PART ONE

The Nature of Spiritual Forces

The Word of God is the king of words and its pervasive (spreading) influence is incalculable. It hath ever dominated and will continue to dominate the realm of being. *Bahá'u'lláh*[1]

Introduction

The unprecedented (no order) energies of our time are spiritual in nature and they result from the coming of God's most recent representative to humankind, the Manifestation of His own light and glory, Bahá'u'lláh (1817–92). As the revealer of God's Word in this age, Bahá'u'lláh has set in motion processes that are creating a new, a divine civilization representing the inevitable destiny of mankind. He has released energies that transform human hearts, shape new social institutions and open up the possibility of a higher order of organization and well-being on earth. In response to this unprecedented outpouring of divine power, negative forces, metaphoric eddies along the banks of this irresistible and swiftly flowing river, have risen in the world around us. This turmoil results from humanity's resistance to the divine purpose and is, therefore, also a consequence of Bahá'u'lláh's Revelation.

The nature of spiritual forces is a prominent theme in the Bahá'í writings, especially those of Shoghi Effendi (1897–1957), Guardian of the Bahá'í Faith. He delineates (outlines) what they are, how they operate in the world and how we can become custodians (keepers) of the forces of light, escaping the influence of the forces of darkness. Through a study of these themes, we gain a clearer vision of the nature of the changes we see taking place in our world and a better sense of our own purpose.

Shoghi Effendi outlines for us the vast spiritual forces of our time. Citing the words of the Báb, he explains that the Báb's spirit is 'vibrating in the innermost realities of all created things'.[2] He then describes this spirit as 'impelling',[3] 'moving',[4] 'world-shaking, world-energizing, world-redeeming',[5] 'world-directing',[6] 'world-vitalizing'[7] and 'all-conquering'.[8] It is a 'God-born Force',[9] 'generative', 'purifying' and 'transmuting' in its 'influence'.[10] Such a force is 'cleansing',[11] 'propelling',[12] 'onrushing',[13] 'intensely alive and all-pervasive'.[14] It is 'irresistible in its sweeping power, incalculable in its potency, unpredictable in its course, mysterious in its working, and awe-inspiring in its manifestations'.[15]

A deliberate and careful study of the Bahá'í writings on spiritual energies reveals that these words are much more than poetic images that stir our hearts: they convey vital principles and laws, systematic processes and insights into the workings of this world. They explain the changes that are taking place and give us a glimpse into our own nature and reality.

This book examines the character of spiritual forces as set forth in the messages of Shoghi Effendi. The opening part of the book presents the patterns of meaning discernible in the full range of his statements referring to 'force', 'energy' and 'power'; the latter part comprises a selection of quotations drawn from the writings of Shoghi Effendi, arranged chronologically, so that readers may consider the ideas in their original context.

The Word of God as the Source of Life

The Bahá'í writings explain that spiritual forces are the foundation of reality, the fundamental basis of life. From a Bahá'í point of view, spirit or spirituality is not just one dimension of human life, it is the motivating impulse of existence, without which nothing can live or move. 'Abdu'l-Bahá uses the image of the sun to illustrate this. Just as the sun is the source of physical existence, the Word of God is the source of human life and civilization. After pointing out that no life would be possible without the warmth and light of the sun, He goes on to say,

> Likewise in the spiritual realm of intelligence and idealism there *(ideas are only reality)* must be a centre of illumination, and that centre is the everlasting, ever-shining Sun, the Word of God . . . Just as the phenomenal sun shines upon the material world producing life and growth, likewise, the spiritual or prophetic Sun confers illumination upon the human world of thought and intelligence, and unless it rose upon the horizon of human existence, the kingdom of man would become dark and extinguished.[16]

Far more than holy scripture to be read and left upon a page, the Word of God is the source of light and life, and separation from it is darkness and death. As will be explained in chapter 2, it is the reality of the Manifestation of God, His power pervading the world, which creates and shapes the individual and gives life to humankind.

Spirit Has Many Names and Functions

A key to understanding spiritual reality is the concept that Spirit is one, even though we often distinguish the separate functions it performs and call them by different names. In the Persian Súriy-i-Ra'ís, Bahá'u'lláh explains that the soul, mind, spirit, heart, sight and hearing of human beings are all one thing. They are 'but one single reality'[17] but are characterized with different names according to the function they perform. In other words, it is the spirit, or soul, that sees through the eyes and hears through the ears. The latter are simply instruments. The spirit is the hearer. The spirit is the seer. The spirit is the knower.

The same complexity applies to the higher divine spirit; all the names and characterizations of divine energy are one but they are spoken of in different ways according to the manner in which they act. In one case, we speak of the will of God, in another of the grace of God, but these are as one reality. They are the refractions of the same light in the different orders of life. We see this in Shoghi Effendi's explanations of the power of Bahá'u'lláh's Revelation in the world. He identifies it first of all as spirit itself. In the opening pages of *God Passes By* he speaks about this spirit which has burst upon the century, and then he characterizes it in various ways: as spirit itself, as the force or forces, as energy, creative energy, as the bounty of God or the grace of God. All of these refer to one divine spirit, which is being expressed by different facets. In the following pages, these terms are used interchangeably.

A familiar passage that illustrates how spiritual power can have many different names is found in the Tablet on love in *Selections from the Writings of 'Abdu'l-Bahá.*[18] There 'Abdu'l-Bahá describes the cohesive power in the universe and calls it love. It is the power holding the planets in their orbits – the cohesive force and connective tissue between everything. Love unites, composes and sustains all things. When love ceases to act on any thing, or if a thing moves itself out of the influence of that love, it becomes decomposed, disunited and discordant. 'Abdu'l-Bahá might have called this the power of unity, or the power of attraction, or divine energy; the name is not the point. Our understanding of spiritual forces is enhanced when we concentrate on trying to understand the systems and processes through which they function in the world.

Spirit is Expressed in Every Dimension of Reality

Another profound and important tool for investigating spiritual reality is the awareness that spiritual truths are expressed at every level of creation. There is a crossover between truths at one level of being and those at another level of being, so that if we understand a relationship or pattern of physical reality, we will find that the same relationship exists not only in varying instances within the physical world itself but also, in a higher set of circumstances, in the spiritual realm. Knowledge of nature and spiritual knowledge are essentially the same thing because the physical world that scientists study can be seen as an expression of spirit – as tangible reflections of spiritual truths.

'Abdu'l-Bahá describes the universality of spirit in all the levels of existence, explaining that each new degree adds to the capacities

Human Beings have cohesion reproduction/growth, sexes, and soul.
Does the spirit world continue with this growth process

THE NATURE OF SPIRITUAL FORCES

of the level below it.[19] Spirit is expressed in the mineral kingdom through the power of cohesion, in the vegetable kingdom through the power of growth and reproduction, in the animal kingdom through sensorial powers. The power of the human kingdom is the rational soul, which can reflect divine spirit in all its aspects. Human beings are the highest expression of spirit, short of the Manifestation of God. Within each level of these progressive expressions of spirit there are also infinite stages of development; carbon atoms, for example, can be found in each of the kingdoms described above and, within the mineral, express 'the power of cohesion'[20] either as a piece of coal or as a diamond. The physical world is an expression, a demonstration, of spiritual reality. Though material, it also is a world of God.

The laws and principles of God govern reality on all levels and we can generalize our knowledge in either direction, higher or lower. Gravity or magnetism, for example, can also be thought of as divine love. Another example is the relationship of the soul to the body. The soul enlivens and sustains the body. On a higher level, the same relationship exists between the Holy Spirit and the human race as a whole. The soul vitalizes the human body; the Holy Spirit, that is the spirit coming from the Manifestation, vitalizes the body of human society. This insight can then be taken to another level where the all-encompassing reality of the universal Manifestation of God is itself animated by the Essence of Divinity.

When in the Hidden Words Bahá'u'lláh asks, 'Know ye not why We created you all from the same dust?'[21] there are undoubtedly multiple levels of meaning but amongst these is also the simple physical reality that all known life is composed for the most part of the same elemental dust – oxygen, hydrogen, nitrogen and carbon. Matter decomposes and is recomposed infinitely such that when we eat and breathe we are quite literally taking in elements of one same substance. This sentiment is similarly expressed in Genesis 3:19, 'In the sweat of thy face shalt thou eat bread, till thou return unto the ground; for out of it wast thou taken: for dust thou art, and unto dust shalt thou return.'

Patterns have varied meanings at different stages of existence.

By learning and investigating the truths at one level, we can, so to speak, ascend the ladder of reality and discover things about the relationships existing in higher realms. As we investigate the operation of spiritual forces in the world, we will encounter truths that have validity at many different levels of reality.

Our exploration, then, of the forces at work in the world will be greatly assisted if we keep in mind that the Word of God is the source of life, that the Bahá'í writings use many terms and images to explain spiritual reality, and that physical science and spiritual learning illuminate each other.

Each divine Revelation is more than teachings, words and a holy book. The words of a Manifestation of God release a spiritual energy, which suffuses the world and remains latent in human creation, ready for activation. The process of revealing the Word of God has a powerful influence on the Manifestation of God Himself as the impact of revelation strikes His soul and He becomes the instrument through which this energy is released into the world. This process is the topic of chapter 2.

Through His Revelation, Bahá'u'lláh has impregnated the world with the creative forces and energies destined to produce a divine civilization. These are not just the 'push' kind of forces that we think of in the world, like rpm or horsepower; they are society-building forces. Spiritual forces are patterned energy, a configuration; they have a form. When we become submissive to that divinely ordained form latent within our being, it begins to crystallize into new patterns of thought and behaviour and, on a collective level, into institutions and the structures of a new society. This process of the crystallization of spiritual forces is considered in chapter 3.

The power of the Revelation of Bahá'u'lláh becomes apparent in the world gradually, as human capacities to receive it develop. The release of spiritual forces continues after the passing away of the outer form of the Manifestation of God, through the institutions of the Covenant, the Administrative Order and other agencies of the Faith. In chapter 4 we consider the progressive release of such spiritual energy and power through these channels.

Chapter 5 examines the turmoil that inevitably accompanies

a new Revelation. The Word of God is an irresistible force: those who conform to it are vitalized by its energies and those who attempt to resist it find old patterns of action no longer workable and witness their disintegration.

Forces of darkness identified by Shoghi Effendi in his writings are analysed in chapter 6. We consider how forces of darkness emerge and what effect they have on the world. Strategies for combatting these negative energies include honest recognition of the influence of dark forces within ourselves. We can subdue them through active reliance on the power of Bahá'u'lláh, through spiritual discipline and by refusing to allow ourselves to think negatively. These strategies are discussed in chapter 7.

An exploration of how to harness the forces of light for our individual and, in turn, societal transformation is found in chapter 8. 'Abdu'l-Bahá in the Tablets of the Divine Plan exhorts us to become incarnate light; we will examine how we can embody the light of God in our lives and in our service to others.

2

The Outpouring of Creative Forces

Verily, the Word of God is the Cause which hath preceded the contingent world – a world which is adorned with the splendours of the Ancient of Days, yet is being renewed and regenerated at all times. *Bahá'u'lláh*[1]

God Himself is the ultimate source of all forces and, with the dawn of this dispensation, Bahá'u'lláh is His agent or the mediator of those forces at work in this world. Shoghi Effendi defines the Faith of Bahá'u'lláh as 'that priceless gem of Divine Revelation, enshrining the Spirit of God and incarnating His Purpose for mankind in this age'.[2] The Manifestation of God, as was also the case in past religious dispensations, is the fountainhead from which the vitalizing energies of revelation continually flow to humanity. In this chapter we examine these forces and how they are released into our world.

Primal Will: The Incarnation of God's Purpose

Primal will is defined in the Bahá'í writings as the first creation of God, the first emanation from the Supreme Essence. It is a vast ocean of potentiality, with nothing in it yet distinguishable. Through the command and purpose and intention of God it resolves its own substance into the form and nature of all created things. Bahá'u'lláh expresses this when stating that 'the letters B and E have been joined and knit together'[3] in the divine command 'Be!' In Arabic these letters are '*kaf*' and '*nun*', which together make the imperative 'kun', meaning 'be' or 'do'. The Guardian rendered these letters in English as 'B' and 'E'. The 'B' has been identified with the primal will and the 'E' with the divine purpose, which is the subsequent stage of unfoldment. The first emanation from God is this primal will, the first will. Divine purpose issues forth from divine will, and together, we are told, they give rise to all the worlds and to the endless generations of souls in the infinite realms of God.

This universal spiritual substance shapes itself into worlds and systems of worlds. It progressively gives rise to this outer physical realm, as well as to the unseen realms of God, which are likewise part of His creation. 'Abdu'l-Bahá refers to the primal will as that universal reality which begets the connections between all created things. He describes this primal will, the will of God, in nearly identical terms with nature and religion.[4] The implications of these overlapping definitions are mysterious and profound but the matter is greatly simplified through the identification of certain root principles.

Spirit does not proceed from matter; matter is generated by spirit. Matter in a sense is a kind of coagulation or condensation of spirit. It becomes solidified, like water freezing into ice, which appears to be something different from water but really is not. Is matter energy or is energy matter? Are not matter and energy essentially the same thing? While matter has laws at its own level, it is equally the incarnation of God's will and purpose.

Bahá'u'lláh, in His supreme mirroring of the divine, is the Sun of Reality, the source of life. In one explanation 'Abdu'l-Bahá refers to the divine bestowals as the sea and human beings as the fish within that sea from which all sustenance comes.[5] We each have a limited reality in our relation to the universal reality of the Manifestation. We are something that is encompassed by it and we receive our life from it. Bahá'u'lláh explains the relationship of creation to the Manifestation of God in the Kitáb-i-Íqán: 'Through Him all things live, move, and have their being.'[6] Everything is sustained by the universal will of the Manifestation of God, which is God's will manifested through Him and operating in the worlds of creation.

There is a depth to this subject which can often be missed when reading familiar quotations. Reflect on the dynamic implications of the following description of the functions of the Word of God:

> Naught but the celestial potency of the Word of God, which ruleth and transcendeth the realities of all things, is capable of harmonizing the divergent thoughts, sentiments, ideas, and convictions of the children of men. Verily, it is the penetrating power in all things, the mover of souls and the binder and regulator in the world of humanity.[7]

Each phrase in this statement explains something essential about existence. The Word of God rules the realities of all things. It is the penetrating power in all things. It holds everything in order and is the binding force among all things, the regulator of the world of humanity.

Bahá'u'lláh is, Himself, the Word of God. His texts are the revealed Book and He is the 'Living Book'.[8] He is the Manifestation of that invisible realm, the primal will, the world of command. He embodies spirit in this world in an all-encompassing manner. The first proof of His Revelation is the person of the Manifestation – the fact that such a being has come into existence.[9] The second proof is the power of the Revelation that pours forth from Him. Bahá'u'lláh then makes a distinction between that Revelation and the message it contains. The Word of God is simultaneously the message contained in the words and the power of the Revelation itself, the energy and divine force for the accomplishment of whatever that Word proclaims and ordains.

Creative Powers of the Word of God

Nothing issues from the mouth of God without at the same time the power for its accomplishment also being released into the world of existence. When Bahá'u'lláh reveals words, forces are released along with those words for the accomplishment of whatever it is that He utters. On one level specific words are spoken and are written down on paper. On another level the means are released for the fulfilment of those words. The power of the Word of God is unimaginable and, but for divine grace, would be beyond our ability to bear:

> Should the Word be allowed to release suddenly all the energies latent within it, no man could sustain the weight of so mighty a Revelation.[10]

Again, the power of the Word is immense: 'holy and never-ending evidences of unimaginable splendour' have appeared and 'oceans of eternal light'[11] have poured forth from every Manifestation of God. This power could 'enable a speck of floating dust to generate, in less than a twinkling of an eye, suns of infinite, of unimaginable splendour, to cause a dewdrop to develop into vast and number-less oceans, to infuse into every letter such a force as to empower it to unfold all the knowledge of past and future ages'.[12]

Vitalizing energy streams out from the Manifestation of God. And the forces released in this Revelation, we are told, are unparal-leled in all religious history. Shoghi Effendi states that the ministry of Bahá'u'lláh is one

> which, by virtue of its creative power, its cleansing force, its healing influences, and the irresistible operation of the world-directing, world-shaping forces it released, stands unparalleled in the religious annals of the entire human race.[13]

The measure of divine light that Bahá'u'lláh has been commis-sioned to release is greater than that of any previous Manifestation of God because this is the time that God has preordained for the maturity, the coming of age of the human race. In his message 'The Goal of a New World Order', Shoghi Effendi affirms that 'nothing short of a power that is born of God' can succeed in establishing the oneness of mankind.[14] This very critical stage in the growth of civilization requires an unprecedented infusion of spiritual energy. The Revelations of the Báb (1819–50) and Bahá'u'lláh, the twin founders of the Faith of God in this day, have endowed the human race with the capacity to attain maturity and to transform civi-lization. When the Báb declared His mission and Mullá Ḥusayn accepted Him, a 'dynamic process, divinely propelled, possessed of undreamt-of potentialities, world-embracing in scope, world-transforming in its ultimate consequences' was set in motion.[15] Referring to the Báb, Shoghi Effendi states, that He

> . . . released, through His coming, the creative energies which, reinforced by the effusions of a swiftly succeeding and infinitely mightier Revelation, were to instil into the entire human race the capacity to achieve its organic unification, attain maturity and thereby reach the final stage in its age-long evolution.[16]

Unity and peace are inevitable because of the capacity with which Bahá'u'lláh and the Báb have endowed the world. If they had not ordained and simultaneously empowered us to grow in this way, a united world would not be possible.

Spiritual energies create capacity. Bahá'u'lláh declares: '. . . We have, at the bidding of the omnipotent Ordainer, breathed a new life into every human frame, and instilled into every word a fresh potency.'[17] His creative energy has instilled into humanity the capacity for attaining a new stage in its development. This makes quite a contrast with the usual way of viewing evolution or the appearance of a divine Manifestation, and it is a particularly appropriate explanation for the times in which we are living. It is clearly much more descriptive and dynamic than saying, 'The Prophets came, they gave holy books and they explained their teachings, and the people listened, believed and tried to obey these teachings, and when they lived by the divine teachings, well then, that made things better in the world.' Shoghi Effendi describes the process in meticulous language of great vitality. Referring to Baghdad during Bahá'u'lláh's residence there, he wrote, 'Above its horizon burst forth the rays of the Sun of Truth,'[18] and 'From it radiated, wave after wave', of 'power', 'radiance' and 'glory'.[19] A literature was being built up in those early days of the Revelation but, more importantly, forces were being released into the world. Waves of power, of radiance and of glory have encompassed the human race as a result of the presence of the Manifestation of God in this world of creation. They have imbued the world with capacity and power. It is our obligation to share access to this power with all humanity. Without it, people have no reason to hope for a better future.

The Process of Divine Revelation

Through divine revelation the forces of the higher world penetrate the realities of this world. There is a kind of a pulsation, a moving from the spiritual plane to the physical and back again. Bahá'u'lláh would receive a spiritual power from the higher invisible realm, which was His animating principle. It would stir His whole being. He would communicate that spiritual power in the form of divine verses, which He would recite or chant. Those verses would thus become physical: through His chanting they would become sound that would reverberate out into space, influencing every atom of existence. They also would be noted down in a written form on a tangible, material page. They reach us in printed form a hundred or more years later; we read them and are able through their influence to connect with the impulses of the original spiritual Revelation of Bahá'u'lláh. These energies impel us to act in conformity with the verses we read. Yet to outward seeming they are no more than black scratchings on a sheet of paper. Spirit has become matter and yet somehow retains and conveys its original spiritual impact. This is indeed a mysterious process.

The little that we know about the experience of the Manifestations when receiving revelation enhances our awareness of the awesome power of the Word of God. Shoghi Effendi likened Bahá'u'lláh's description of 'the impact of the onrushing force of the Divine Summons upon His entire being' to 'the vision of God that caused Moses to fall in a swoon, and the voice of Gabriel which plunged Muḥammad into such consternation that, hurrying to the shelter of His home, He bade His wife, Khadíjih, envelop Him in His mantle'.[20] For the first time, with Bahá'u'lláh's coming, we have an authentic description from the Manifestation of God Himself regarding this experience of receiving revelation.

During the days I lay in the prison of Ṭihrán, though the galling weight of the chains and the stench-filled air allowed Me but little sleep, still in those infrequent moments of slumber I felt as if something flowed from the crown of My head over My breast, even as a mighty torrent that precipitateth itself upon the earth from the summit of a lofty mountain. Every limb of My body would, as a result, be set afire. At such moments My tongue recited what no man could bear to hear.[21]

The recollections of early believers inform us that Bahá'u'lláh would usually dismiss the friends from His presence at a time of revelation because the power of it was so intense that they could not bear it. Even His secretaries, who had been endowed by Bahá'u'lláh with capacity to note down the verses, would sometimes swoon away under the influence of the descent of the Word. The force of divine revelation was truly overwhelming.

Bahá'u'lláh explained the transcendent experience of revelation in images that could be understood by His followers. He described His first intimation of revelation as a dream in which 'exalted words were heard on every side'.[22] In another passage He elaborated:

While engulfed in tribulations I heard a most wondrous, a most sweet voice, calling above My head. Turning My face, I beheld a Maiden – the embodiment of the remembrance of the name of My Lord – suspended in the air before Me. So rejoiced was she in her very soul that her countenance shone with the ornament of the good pleasure of God, and her cheeks glowed with the brightness of the All-Merciful. Betwixt earth and heaven she was raising a call which captivated the hearts and minds of men. She was imparting to both My inward and outer being tidings which rejoiced My soul, and the souls of God's honoured servants.

Pointing with her finger unto My head, she addressed all who are in heaven and all who are on earth, saying: By God! This is the Best-Beloved of the worlds, and yet ye comprehend not. This is the Beauty of God amongst you, and the power of His sovereignty within you, could ye but understand.[23]

Shoghi Effendi writes that the end of Bahá'u'lláh's first imprisonment was marked by 'the sudden eruption of the forces released by an overpowering, soul-revolutionizing Revelation'[24] and that later, in Baghdad, Bahá'u'lláh 'increasingly experienced, and progressively communicated to His future followers, the onrushing influences of its [His Revelation's] informing force.'[25]

Finally, the physical death of the divine Messenger is another step in the progressive release of heavenly forces: it widens the scope of His influence. After He is freed from those earthly limitations to which He subjects Himself by coming to this physical world, He is free to pour out an even greater grace on the human race from His invisible realm. As Shoghi Effendi explains with regard to the soul of Bahá'u'lláh in that new stage:

> Its influence no longer circumscribed by any physical limitations, its radiance no longer beclouded by its human temple, that soul could henceforth energize the whole world to a degree unapproached at any stage in the course of its existence on this planet.[26]

In this chapter we have considered several deep and profoundly important subjects. The essence of life, the force that gives shape to reality, is the primal will of God. The Manifestation of God expresses God's will in the world, and we live and move and have our being in His reality. The words revealed by the Báb and Bahá'u'lláh have a regenerative power that brings into existence a new creation. Chapters 3 and 4 explain the progressive and ongoing effect of divine revelation on the world.

3

The Crystallization of Divine Forces

... the Word of God hath infused such awesome power into the
inmost essence of humankind that He hath stripped men's human
qualities of all effect, and hath, with His all-conquering might,
unified the peoples in a vast sea of oneness. *'Abdu'l-Bahá*[1]

Transformed human beings and a spiritual civilization come
into being when people respond to the vitalizing, propelling
forces and creative energies that are released into the world by
the Manifestation of God. Divine revelation sets the pattern and
creates the potential, which is the first essential step. Next is for
humanity to conform to that pattern. Shoghi Effendi likens this
to a process of crystallization, saying that the spirit released by
Bahá'u'lláh gradually crystallizes into new institutions and a new
society. This is the distinguishing feature of the Formative Age
of the Bahá'í era. In this chapter we consider precise definitions
of this process, the meaning of the image of crystallization, the
Covenant and the Administrative Order as examples of the crystallization of spirit, and how the process works in the life of society
and its individual members.

For any spirit or ideal to operate in society it needs a material,
manifest form. Having a belief in the high value of education does
not of itself educate children. While that ideal is an essential component of such a process, education also requires the provision
of teachers, a location for the teaching to take place, educational
materials and so on. Without these the ideal of education cannot
become a reality in this world. The spirit released by Bahá'u'lláh
has to have a tangible vehicle so that it can fulfil its purpose. A

divine order is now latent in creation. It was engendered by the Báb and Bahá'u'lláh in their plan for a new social order and in the energies they released for its accomplishment. The course this world society must follow, we are told, is already fixed and immutable. It will appear in the world by degrees, as we allow these forces to inform our being, as we sacrifice our lower selves to this higher reality, reflect it in our daily lives and begin to draw it into human affairs, and in these ways solidify its principles, its design and its pattern.

At the beginning of the study of spiritual forces which ultimately led to this book, quotations from the Guardian about this process at first seemed like imaginative examples of his incredible mastery of English prose. Along with all the other quotations about spiritual forces, they were placed in chronological order in a looseleaf notebook. As the study continued, it became clear that over a 20-year period Shoghi Effendi had written in a consistent way about the concept of spiritual power crystallizing into the structures of a new civilization. Beginning with a letter written in 1926, then again in the World Order letters written in the 1930s, in *God Passes By* in 1944 and in later messages to Bahá'í communities he used the same concept and terminology. As these quotations were systematically collected and studied they revealed that he was not just offering us a beautiful and powerful image; he was setting out a fundamental principle of spiritual reality.

The following selections express the concept of crystallizing spiritual forces that recurs throughout the Guardian's writings:

> The onrushing forces so miraculously released through the agency of two independent and swiftly successive Manifestations are now under our very eyes and through the care of the chosen stewards of a far-flung Faith being gradually mustered and disciplined. They are slowly crystallizing into institutions that will come to be regarded as the hall-mark and glory of the age we are called upon to establish and by our deeds immortalize.[2]

> . . . this healing Agency, this leavening Power, this cementing Force, intensely alive and all-pervasive, has been taking shape, is

crystallizing into institutions, is mobilizing its forces, and is preparing for the spiritual conquest and the complete redemption of
mankind.[3]

Though the Heroic Age of His Faith is passed, the creative energies which that Age has released have not as yet crystallized into
that world society which, in the fullness of time, is to mirror forth
the brightness of His glory.[4]

We learn from these quotations that revelation sets in motion
a profound chain of events. The forces released by the Báb and
Bahá'u'lláh are being 'gradually mustered and disciplined';[5] they
are 'taking shape'[6] but they 'have not as yet'[7] attained their final
form. These forces are 'crystallizing' into the institutions of the
Faith in the Formative Age, institutions that will be used for the
'spiritual conquest and the complete redemption of mankind.'[8]
This system, which is coming into being in this transitional stage
of the Faith, will reach its fruition in the Golden Age. In the future,
that 'intensely alive and all-pervasive'[9] power will be expressed in
the form of a society that will mirror the full brightness of the
light of revelation. Institutions ordained by Bahá'u'lláh, including
Spiritual Assemblies, the Nineteen Day Feast, the law of consultation, the institution of the learned and so on, are destined to
become ever-greater crystallizations of His spirit. The present-day
institute process offers another clear example of this development. It is not only the institutions of the Faith but beyond them
a whole new society – including its attitudes, patterns of interaction, and social structures – that will come to 'mirror' the light
of Bahá'u'lláh. We see this in various mass movements aligned
indirectly with His intentions. The basic agent of this transformation is the individual soul. The divine initiative requires a human
response to give it a material existence, to give it concrete reality
in this world.

Spirit incarnates itself in the material world when souls and
communities of souls reach out to the Revelation and strive
to align themselves with it and incorporate it into their being.
Through our efforts, through our vision, through our spiritual

discipline, such as obedience to the laws of prayer and fasting, we equip ourselves to be instruments attracting and channelling this energy for the good of human society. It happens as Bahá'í institutions develop the capacity to make decisions and act in ways that express Bahá'u'lláh's purpose. It happens gradually as a society's ways of thinking and acting change through interaction with His words and the energies He has released.

Crystallizing Spiritual Energy

Crystallization is a powerful and appropriate image for the creation of a spiritual civilization. A quartz crystal can be transparent or translucent. It refracts, reflects and captures light. Most rock does not allow light in. A slab of limestone or slate is opaque but light is drawn through a quartz crystal. If Bahá'í institutions and the structures of society are crystalline like quartz, they will contain and radiate divine light; they will be instruments for the forces of light.

Crystals conform to infinite geometric shapes. They follow a unified pattern that varies only in minor details. Many of us are familiar with one common example of this. Particles of moisture are attracted to each other in the upper atmosphere and coalesce into a droplet that, once it hits cold air, becomes a microscopic ice crystal. This tiny crystal attracts to itself more water molecules, which also crystallize, soon growing into a beautiful snowflake. Each snowflake is unique but follows the universal pattern of snowflakes. It is perfect. What but divine providence could have designed such perfection? Institutions and social structures share this quality of almost geometric regularity when they conform to the laws and principles of Bahá'u'lláh. The Word of God and the law of God are the predetermined pattern. As people associate with each other according to the spiritual laws of the Faith, in love, in unity and interdependence, that association increasingly reflects spiritual reality; it gives outer form to that wonderfully beneficent reality.

Crystals are aggregated from a large number of smaller units, all of which have the same basic shape. This is also true of the Bahá'í institutions we are building. Before the institutions come together, their composite individuals should ideally be striving to conform themselves to the laws and principles of Bahá'u'lláh, such that the spiritual structure of the individual units might lock together harmoniously and in unity. Because of their geometric regularity, crystals are strong and tough; they can withstand pressure. They cannot be broken easily. Universal obedience to spiritual laws and to the teachings of the Faith will give Bahá'í institutions and communities exceptional strength and resilience.

In the process of crystallization, a change in energy or pressure causes a substance which has been in a state of relative dispersion to reorganize at a higher level of order. For example, when a liquid cools it gets to a certain point where it crystallizes according to fixed laws; it changes state. It is not possible to see the pattern that is coming but it is suddenly there. This is perhaps one of the greatest images of spirit 'becoming matter'. As was mentioned previously, think of the difference in form between water and ice. Ice is water and yet it is not, since ice conforms to a pattern – most easily seen as the cooling process begins – and is solid, while water is less firmly structured. The World Order which Bahá'u'lláh has ordained, and which Bahá'ís are endeavouring to create, is His spirit crystallized – made tangible and incarnate – in the world.

Before they take visible shape, both the design for the human body and the design for future human society already exist in a higher realm and gradually imprint themselves on malleable, receptive matter as capacity is developed. One remembers a nearly universal science lesson from the early years of school, in which the teacher puts a magnet under a piece of paper onto which small iron filings are scattered. The unseen energetic influence of the magnet overpowers the inertia of the iron particles and visibly imprints itself upon them. The many disorganized tiny fragments are mysteriously moved from their original positions by this force of attraction and drawn into the pattern determined by the magnet. Logic would seem to indicate that something similar, but infinitely more complex, happens from the very beginnings of embryonic life in the womb. Some mysterious force causes a coming together of elements in a specific pattern, the migration of atoms of carbon and oxygen and calcium through the placenta and into the precise places where they are needed for the formation of the new organism. As the first primitive cells multiply, soon they begin to differentiate, one type becoming part of a vital organ, another type a tiny fingernail. And just as is the case with the snowflakes, each individual body created by this amazing demonstration of unseen energies at work is, at one and the same time, unique and very much like the others of its species.

The gifts of the spirit, the talents and powers of the spirit, call for an agency through which they can operate. They give rise to an appropriate instrument for their expression in human society. In past millennia, family and tribal units, city-states and finally nations came into being in this way, as higher and higher expressions of spiritual capacity. In our time Bahá'u'lláh's blessing of establishing the Kingdom of God across the whole earth requires, as citizens for that Kingdom, souls who are willing to embrace that spirit. The cooperating, conforming elements are these individuals striving to embody the will of God in their personal lives, as well as Bahá'í institutions expressing His will in their actions and corporate identities and in new social structures. These patterns of thinking and behaviour begin to manifest themselves with the gradual rising of the sun of revelation. The energy that feeds this process could be viewed as 'configured'; it has an inherent design and pattern to it. The Word of God creates the potentialities for its own accomplishment. It provides the energy and the design for what Bahá'u'lláh has revealed. This 'onrushing force' of revelation seeks receptive souls and communities through which it can operate.

Crystallization of Spiritual Forces in Human Hearts

Bahá'u'lláh explains that the infusion of His spirit into humankind causes the material world to reflect the divine world: 'A race of men, incomparable in character, shall be raised up . . .'[10] Invisible spiritual forces transform those human beings who are desirous of change, bringing them out of their negligence into a wakeful spiritual state in which they become the active and welcoming instruments of these blessed higher energies. Their minds are imbued with divine truths, with the spiritual principles, with the precepts, the laws, the teachings of the Faith, and these begin to animate such individuals with fresh life. The new race of men is composed of those who respond to and are impelled forward in conformity with the will of God.

'Abdu'l-Bahá expressed this wish when He said, 'God willing, this terrestrial world may become as a celestial mirror upon which we may behold the imprint of the traces of Divinity, and the fundamental qualities of a new creation may be reflected from the reality of love shining in human hearts.'[11]

The spiritual forces emanating from Bahá'u'lláh crystallize first in individual human consciousness – and then afterwards, as a result, that crystallization extends into the outside world and becomes manifest in visible institutions, such as the Mashriqu'l-Adhkár, the Bahá'í House of Worship. This happens through our will, through our intention, through our dedication to using divine energies in the manner specified by the Word of God. The effect of the energy which the Revelation releases into society is at first diffuse and in a sense undisciplined. Though some individuals are more aware of it than are others, everyone on earth is affected by this force. Those who are able to identify its source can begin to align their individual actions and voluntarily conform to the requirements of the Cause of God. One can become more and more of a channel for the release of this energy in a way that is focused, purposeful and ordered. We channel this energy towards specific tasks, using it to propagate the Faith, to solve social problems, to draw ourselves into closer relationship or conformity with the Revelation, to increase our intuition, our penetration and understanding of spiritual matters.

This crystallization of spiritual forces in the lives of people is an essential meaning of consolidation – making the Bahá'í community solid. When we are first attracted and awakened as believers, the Word of God may have a rather diffuse influence on us. These ideals and principles become increasingly constant in us as we allow the power of the Revelation to act on our character. Each one of us acquires those attitudes towards God which cause the gem-like reality of the soul to begin to shine in all of its facets with the radiance of Bahá'u'lláh. This enlightenment is developed through our daily interactions with the Word of God and its divine prescriptions.

Through this individual illumination we are attracted to the spirit in each other, and the crystalline units of human souls align themselves, together, in the patterns preordained by Bahá'u'lláh, producing light upon light. This cordial and revitalizing spirit of attraction contributes indispensably to the effectiveness of the agencies of the Faith – National and Local Spiritual Assemblies, the Nineteen Day Feasts, committees, training institutes, as well as Counsellors, the Auxiliary Boards and others.

The Covenant and Creative Energies

One of the primary crystallizations of the forces released by Bahá'u'lláh was the establishment of His Covenant, the appointment of 'Abdu'l-Bahá as the ordained successor and centre through whom this power would be distributed or channelled to the world.

After the passing of Bahá'u'lláh an instrument was necessary to safeguard the unity of the community and to canalize the forces released by the Twin Manifestations of God. That instrument was the Covenant of Bahá'u'lláh and after it followed the 'Child of the Covenant' – the divinely ordained Administrative Order. Shoghi Effendi describes how this Order was engendered by the impact of the creative forces or energies released by revelation, acting on the mind and spirit of 'Abdu'l-Bahá.[12] These forces later gave birth to 'this supreme, this infallible Organ for the accomplishment of a Divine Purpose.'[13] The Will and Testament of 'Abdu'l-Bahá, the 'Charter' of the 'New World Order',[14] radiates the forces necessary for the fruition of both the Formative and the Golden Ages of the Bahá'í dispensation.

The release of creative energies and the formation of powerful spiritual tools follow each other in a cyclical pattern. It began when Bahá'u'lláh released incalculable spiritual forces through the word He both revealed and embodied. These forces eventually crystallized into an instrument. This instrument was His Covenant, the promise that divine authority and protection would flow to the believers through 'Abdu'l-Bahá and His guidance. The very Covenant itself, as it began to operate, released new forces which gave birth to another stage in the Cause, the Administrative Order. The forces of the Administrative Order, as they develop and consolidate their capacity to express the spiritual verities of the invisible world in the visible world, release further energies. These will then give rise to the birth of the World Order of Bahá'u'lláh, which could be described as the socio-political embodiment of Bahá'u'lláh's Revelation. As the institutions of the World Order mature and develop, as they become purer and more expansive channels of spirit, they will increasingly release the sublime energies that will give birth to the promised world civilization. The solidification of spiritual forces at each stage in this process makes it possible for the next one to commence.

Crystallization of Spiritual Forces as the Administrative Order

Studying this process helps us to understand Shoghi Effendi's statement that the Bahá'í system is entirely unique among systems of government.[15] These are institutions, vehicles and agencies through which the Manifestation of God is present in human society – through which He guides, informs and shapes human affairs. This is not government of the people by the people, or by a group who reserve power for themselves, or by an elite body that claims to be the representative of God. It is an incarnation of the spirit breathed by Bahá'u'lláh upon the world and a channel through which the vitalizing energy of His Revelation can flow. The Bahá'í system combines positive elements of the world's systems of government but embodies a power which is lacking in all of them – the divine spirit of Bahá'u'lláh. It has elements of democracy but Bahá'í elections take place in a rarefied atmosphere of supplication and devotion to God in which any hint of partisanship is anathema and those elected to Assemblies are responsible to God and to their conscience rather than to those who elect them. Every institution that He has ordained is a channel for His spirit. Through them 'the dynamic forces latent in the Faith can unfold, crystallize, and shape the lives and conduct of men . . .'[16]

26

The entity being created as the Bahá'í Administrative Order is an aggregate of spiritual relationships, a network of mutual spiritual attractions among the members of a community, their representatives and their Lord. Each unit in the system – each individual and each elected body – works to reflect the qualities and attributes of God. As the elements of the system interact, they draw out and enhance the divine qualities in the other units of the system. The interaction of a community and an Assembly is infinitely more than the carrying out of village, town or national business – it is a spiritual reciprocity. Thus Spiritual Assemblies become 'the potent sources of the progress of man', from which 'the spirit of life streameth in every direction'.[17] In its letter on freedom the Universal House of Justice wrote that the pattern of interaction of institutions and individuals depends on love, 'the recognition of a mutuality of benefits, and on the spirit of cooperation maintained by the willingness, the courage, the sense of responsibility, and the initiative of individuals – these being expressions of their devotion and submission to the will of God'.[18]

Crystallization of Spiritual Forces in the Structures of Society

Commonly held and pervasive patterns of thought are part of the character of any society. Ways of thinking about life that are common to a culture – its well-worn mental habits – have a deep influence on what a society does and how people act. For example, a society that holds the belief that life is a competitive struggle for existence will organize its economy, its educational system, its social services and its provision for security in very different ways from a society that holds the belief that mutual service and reciprocity are essential characteristics of living beings. The conviction that humans are merely sophisticated animals leads to principles of commerce, government and law that are very different from those that flow from the conviction that human beings have a capacity to reflect the qualities of God, which can only unfold through a conscious act of will. Ideas – bad ones as well as good ones – are expressed in the structures and patterns of a society.

New social structures and new patterns of organization emerge as understanding of the Word of God permeates society. The process of crystallization takes place at the level of principles, social structures and communal beliefs, as well as in the hearts of individuals and in the administrative order. Shoghi Effendi, in a statement about economics written on his behalf, makes this clear:

> The primary consideration is the Spirit that has to permeate our economic life and this will gradually crystallize itself into definite institutions and principles that will help to bring about the ideal conditions foretold by Bahá'u'lláh.[19]

Recognizing the power of ideas in the transformation of societies enables us to understand the implications of many of 'Abdu'l-Bahá's statements which encourage people to change the world by changing the way they think. He admonished Americans to manifest 'true economics' by showing love, kindness, severance and generosity.[20] He advocated spiritual strategies for transforming trade and government:

> When you breathe forth the breath of the Holy Spirit from your hearts into the world, commerce and politics will take care of themselves in perfect harmony . . . It is not your work but that of the Holy Spirit which you breathe forth through the Word. This is a fundamental truth.[21]

In this chapter we have examined the significance of Shoghi Effendi's statements about the crystallization of Bahá'u'lláh's spirit into the agencies and institutions of a new World Order. We have seen that this evocative image expresses a fundamental principle of the organization of reality. The pattern of a release of energy, followed by crystallization at a new level of organization, occurs in the physical world, in social structures and in the spiritual realm. The Covenant and Bahá'í administrative institutions are expressions of spiritual forces that will eventually develop into a world civilization. As the creative energies of the Word of God permeate individual souls and then social institutions and structures, the spirit of Bahá'u'lláh increasingly influences the visible world.

The purpose of the Revelation is to make this visible world a mirror of the higher divine realm: the reflection of God's light shines in the soul of each person and in the connections they make with other souls. World Order is not simply having a world currency, tolerating differences and limiting the use of force; World Order implies a transformation within each soul and an entirely new relationship among the peoples of the earth. Without a mutual attraction to God, the delicate mirrors of human hearts are all facing in different directions, so that when the sunlight shines on us it is dispersed as so many divergent rays. If we all face God in the same way, in other words if we all align our lives to the divine teachings and unite under its structures, all of these mirrors will be realigned and we will become one solid, unified reflection. Then will the ineffable image of the Unseen appear with all its glory in the reality of humankind and the long-awaited Kingdom of God on earth come into being.

4

The Progressive Release of Divine Forces

The Word of God may be likened unto a sapling, whose roots have been implanted in the hearts of men. It is incumbent upon you to foster its growth through the living waters of wisdom, of sanctified and holy words, so that its root may become firmly fixed and its branches may spread out as high as the heavens and beyond. *Bahá'u'lláh*[1]

Spiritual energies are released and take effect in the world in a gradual manner. As the light of Bahá'u'lláh is increasingly recognized and the people of the world begin to order their individual and collective lives in response to His words, latent spiritual powers are awakened. Just as the human body grows through progressive stages towards maturity, with particular gifts and strengths appearing at each stage, the fruit of divine revelation also grows through successive stages. As the institutions of the Cause and Bahá'í communities mature, they are able to channel a greater measure of divine forces. In this chapter, we look at Shoghi Effendi's delineation of these stages and consider the release of divine energy through the institutions of the Administrative Order, the teaching plans and the Bahá'í Houses of Worship.

The gradual, progressive release of divine forces implies that what we now experience of the power of Bahá'u'lláh is the merest glimmering of the dawn of His sun. Years ago one of the friends in Europe asked Shoghi Effendi why the world was full of chaos and confusion; she presumed that such disorder was supposed to have happened first and only then Christ could return. The Guardian's response was that Bahá'u'lláh's coming is not just His physical appearance. Rather His coming is that stage of recognition by humanity when He shall be accepted, when His glory shall be manifest in the world – when all eyes shall see Him.

Stages in the Release and Crystallization of Divine Power

Shoghi Effendi uses the words 'infuse', 'diffuse' and 'suffuse' to describe different stages in the propagation of the light of the Word of God. Infusion happens when the divine will instils new capacity and ability within us. At the moment of revelation 'boundless potentialities' are 'infused into the entire body of mankind'.[2] Diffusion of divine light is the initial spread of faith in Bahá'u'lláh throughout the world. The divine light has been diffused and propagated through the teaching efforts of the first travelling teachers who arose, the pioneers and the first believers who established Bahá'í communities all over the planet. With the opening of the former communist countries to the Faith in the 1990s, that process was basically completed. The current focus of Bahá'í activity is to develop human resources systematically so that the Bahá'í community can grow from the phase of spreading everywhere to the point of eliciting a strong, profoundly committed, active response to Bahá'u'lláh among the masses. That is the stage of suffusion and it will occur and continue until the divine light penetrates into the very heart of the nations of the world, until they are fully permeated with the influence of Bahá'u'lláh's Revelation.

Shoghi Effendi alludes to these stages when he calls the Báb's Revelation a 'Holy Seed of infinite preciousness, holding within itself incalculable potentialities'.[3] He describes how this Seed of the Faith is ground in the mill of martyrdom and oppression, but yields an oil

> ... whose first flickering light cast upon the sombre, subterranean walls of the Síyáh-Chál of Ṭihrán, whose fire gathered brilliance in Baghdád and shone in full resplendency in its crystal globe in Adrianople, whose rays warmed and illuminated the fringes of the American, European, Australian continents through the tender ministerings of the Centre of the Covenant, whose radiance is

now overspreading the surface of the globe during the present Formative Age, whose full splendour is destined in the course of future millenniums to suffuse the entire planet.[4]

The successive processes of infusion, diffusion and suffusion are characteristic of the different ages of the Faith. During the Heroic Age, spiritual forces and potentialities were infused into the world when the Báb and Bahá'u'lláh revealed the Word of God. Our age, the Formative or Iron Age, which commenced with the passing of the Master, is the time of the wide diffusion of those forces and the beginning of their systematic effect on society. In this age the Administrative Order has been created, strengthened and spread over the entire planet. It has established the Faith of Bahá'u'lláh in every part of the world. The whole purpose of the Administrative Order is to propagate the Cause so that human souls may drink of the water of life and bring about the transformation in human society that is the promise of our Faith. This Order is the embryonic stage of that World Order which will appear throughout human society as the planet becomes suffused with the message of Bahá'u'lláh. In outlining the nature of the growth of the Faith in the second Bahá'í century, from 1944 to 2044, Shoghi Effendi made reference to the Administrative Order and foreshadowed the movement from diffusion to suffusion:

> The second [Bahá'í] century is destined to witness a tremendous deployment and a notable consolidation of the forces working towards the worldwide development of that Order, as well as the first stirrings of that World Order, of which the present Administrative System is at once the precursor, the nucleus and pattern – an Order which, as it slowly crystallizes and radiates its benign influence over the entire planet, will proclaim at once the coming of age of the whole human race, as well as the maturity of the Faith itself, the progenitor of that Order.[5]

Eventually, in the coming Golden Age, the spiritual forces of the Revelation of Bahá'u'lláh will entirely permeate the planet. The World Order of Bahá'u'lláh will come about as a majority of people in the world embrace the Faith and spontaneously adopt the system of Bahá'u'lláh to structure the affairs of daily life – the civil affairs of society. The Bahá'í writings predict that this will happen in the future, as more and more people become Bahá'ís and eventually the masses of mankind come under the light of the Revelation.

The World Order of Bahá'u'lláh, Bahá'ís believe, will be the fulfilment of the Christian prayer for the coming of the Kingdom of God on earth. It means that humanity will voluntarily come under the governance of God, through the divinely ordained laws and institutions promulgated by Bahá'u'lláh. It is important when we consider the future to keep in mind that these things will come about through humanity's own response to Bahá'u'lláh and not through any coercion. There could never be any forced conversion or any compulsion that people accept Bahá'í law. Our Faith prohibits that, and also – from a purely practical point of view – the forced conversion of any individual would be senseless and self-defeating as it would, by definition, mean that the unwillingness of such a person would nullify his ability to contribute to the unity and strength of the community. The gradual and organic growth of a global civilization based on Bahá'u'lláh's teachings is something we naturally anticipate, arising from the belief that He is a Messenger of God.

Release of Divine Forces through the Administrative Order

Bahá'í Assemblies, Shoghi Effendi has explained, release spiritual forces which endow a nation with new powers and capacities. Although this observation comes in a letter which refers to the Bahá'í Assemblies of North America, in principle it applies to Assemblies all over the world.

> The creative energies, mysteriously generated by the first stirrings of the embryonic World Order of Bahá'u'lláh, have, as soon as released within a nation destined to become its cradle and champion, endowed that nation with the worthiness, and invested it with the powers and capacities, and equipped it spiritually, to play the part foreshadowed in these prophetic words.[6]

Even 'the first stirrings' – the actions of the Assemblies which are the precursors of Bahá'u'lláh's World Order – release powers and capacities to fulfil the will of God for this day.

In another letter the Guardian explains that the initial impulse of a world civilization of the future will come from the same spirit animating today's embryonic institutions of the Faith: 'a civilization destined as it unfolds to derive its initial impulse from the spirit animating the very institutions which, in their embryonic state, are now stirring in the womb of the present Formative Age of the Faith'.[7] In likening Bahá'í institutions to embryos, Shoghi Effendi is again using an image which implies systematic growth and patterned development. The present-day Bahá'í administrative institutions are the 'embryonic' World Order.[8] This embryo is the nucleus for a growing being, and though as yet undeveloped, contains within itself the pattern of that future being.

Bahá'ís are charged with an awesome responsibility, since nations will ultimately derive their capacity and power to carry out the will of God from the actions of Bahá'í institutions. The impulse to create a world civilization will come from those institutions now in an embryonic stage. If there is no embryo, there can be no child. If the embryo is unhealthy, the child's future is compromised. An embryo consists of barely differentiated cells but it holds a plan, it has a future. The capacities it will have in maturity are entirely imperceptible and yet infinitely greater than those it possesses in its embryonic state.

Even in the earliest stages of development Bahá'í administration has a far-reaching role. Shoghi Effendi describes it in thought-provoking terms:

> . . . the community of the Most Great Name, whose world-embracing, continually consolidating activities constitute the one integrating process in a world whose institutions, secular as well as religious, are for the most part dissolving . . .[9]

The ability of the Bahá'ís to come together, to focus on Bahá'u'lláh's pattern for the future of mankind and align ourselves to it, is a source of strength and stability for the planet. These actions advance humanity. Shoghi Effendi cabled regarding a national convention that, 'TO ITS DELEGATES [1937 American Convention] GIVEN GREAT OPPORTUNITY RELEASE FORCES WHICH WILL USHER IN ERA WHOSE SPLENDOUR MUST OUTSHINE HEROIC AGE OUR BELOVED CAUSE . . .'[10] The process of releasing and crystallizing divine energy, and creating new capacities is a continuous one: Shoghi Effendi's messages to the Bahá'í world make it clear that each new achievement and collective endeavour contributes to this ongoing process.

Release of Divine Forces through Systematic Teaching

Teaching the Cause is one of the principal ways through which creative energies and forces continue to be released into the world. The Tablets of the Divine Plan and the successive teaching plans derived from it serve as a vehicle for the propagation of the divine light. In message after message Shoghi Effendi wrote to the believers about the 'propelling force'[11] generated by the Tablets of the Divine Plan; the 'powers released'[12] for the prosecution of a teaching plan; the 'upsurge [of] Bahá'u'lláh's impelling spirit';[13] and the 'potentialities with which the community of the Greatest Name has been so generously and mysteriously endowed by 'Abdu'l-Bahá.'[14] The prosecution of these plans, now generated and directed by the Universal House of Justice, energizes both the Bahá'í community and the individual Bahá'ís. Spiritual energies are released at the inception of a plan to aid in its accomplishment; when we act in accordance with it, our potential is drawn out. When we succeed, we are not just winning the goals – we are opening fresh floodgates of grace. This is why, to a great degree, one plan is dependent on the accomplishment of the previous one.

The same process occurs when an individual adopts a teaching plan. The act of setting a goal releases energy. A decision of will focuses one's inner resources, and when the goal is accomplished, it confirms, dynamizes and enhances the capacity of the group or individual that has set the goal.

Study of Shoghi Effendi's messages, addressed to various Bahá'í communities, helps us gain a clear vision about ourselves, our actions and our world. His writings aptly describe the processes of integration and disintegration characteristic of our time and remain as vital and applicable now as the day they were penned. He tells us who we are, that our potential is to 'be spiritually welded into a unit at once dynamic and coherent, and be suffused with the creative, the directing and propelling forces proceeding from the Source of Revelation Himself, and be made . . . the vehicle of His grace from on high'.[15] He fires us with a vision of what we are doing:

> A community now in the process of marshalling and directing, in such vast territories, in such outlying regions, amidst such a diversity of peoples, at so precarious a stage in the fortunes of mankind, forces of such incalculable potency, to serve purposes so meritorious and lofty, cannot afford to falter for a moment or retrace its steps on the path it now travels.[16]

He tells us what kind of power is available to us: 'the Force which energizes your mission is limitless in its range and incalculable in its potency'.[17]

> The impetus that has been given by the Manifestation of God for this Age is the sole one that can regenerate humanity, and as we Bahá'ís are the only ones yet aware of this new force in the world, our obligation towards our fellow men is tremendous and inescapable![18]

The whole point of teaching is to link individual souls with this force. We are the only ones in the world who are conscious of its existence. We have witnessed its transforming power in our own lives. Teaching announces to people the arrival of this revelation of transforming power to which human souls now have access, on which they can draw and which will infinitely bless them. It is inviting people to release the potential that is latent within their own being.

Release of Divine Power through Bahá'í Houses of Worship

The Bahá'í House of Worship, a divinely ordained institution that instils spiritual power into human affairs, is one of the greatest gifts of Bahá'u'lláh to the world in this day. Called the Mashriqu'l-Adhkár or 'Dawning Place of the Remembrance of God', the House of Worship, according to Bahá'u'lláh's injunction, is a nine-sided place of prayer and meditation, surrounded by dependencies that supply the community's needs for education, health and social well-being.

Spiritual forces converge upon and radiate out from the Mashriqu'l-Adhkár, and the 'higher the degree of our renunciation and self-sacrifice, the wider the range of the contributing believers, the more apparent will become the vitalizing forces that are to emanate from this unique and sacred Edifice . . .'[19]

Visitors to the Houses of Worship occasionally ask why funds have not been used instead to address poverty. While a valid question when considered in the short term alone, the Mashriqu'l-Adhkár represents the sole enduring solution to the ills of humanity – namely the coming together of all humanity (regardless of race, rank or gender) in loving devotion to its common Creator and, radiating out from and based firmly upon this common recognition, the establishment of structures and agencies that can then address the socio-economic needs of humanity.

The essential activities of worshipping God and serving humanity coalesce in the House of Worship complex in a powerful way. Shoghi Effendi has written that, 'Nothing short of direct and constant interaction between the spiritual forces emanating from this House of Worship centring in the heart of the Mashriqu'l-Adhkár, and the energies consciously displayed by those who administer its affairs in their service to humanity can possibly provide the necessary agency capable of removing the ills that have so long and so grievously afflicted humanity.'[20] He tells us that prayer, by itself, produces the fruits of pious worship and the exaltation of the soul; but to have an abiding effect in the world and to transform the conditions of mankind these inner benefits have to be tied to organized service. In other words, in order to accomplish anything we need to have the spiritual forces which come from the Word of God, combined with practical action in service to humanity. This combination alone will succeed.

> For it is assuredly upon the consciousness of the efficacy of the Revelation of Bahá'u'lláh, reinforced on one hand by spiritual communion with His Spirit, and on the other by the intelligent application and faithful execution of the principles and laws He revealed, that the salvation of a world in travail must ultimately depend.[21]

Another letter written on the Guardian's behalf addresses the effect of group prayers: 'He does not believe any radiations of thought or healing, from any group, is going to bring peace. Prayer, no doubt, will help the world, but what it needs is to accept Bahá'u'lláh's system so as to build up the World Order on a new foundation, a divine foundation . . .'[22] Prayer is important but a new divine foundation must also be created.

We see above that the Guardian emphasized the necessary interaction between 'the spiritual forces emanating from this House of Worship' and 'the energies consciously displayed by those who administer its affairs in their service to humanity.'[23] There is a pulsing interaction between the spiritual power of the Mashriqu'l-Adhkár, the divinely-ordained House of Worship where believers are enjoined to gather at dawn to remember and praise their Lord, and that unseen power's outer manifestation through the worshippers' work in the everyday world, especially via the future dependencies of the House of Worship.

Spiritual communion creates a tremendous power which is channelled and released through the House of Worship. Sometimes we feel this in large conferences of believers; the excitement of many souls turning towards God together; the interplay of spirits, the light upon light of the souls of the friends reflecting off each other. Communal worship in the Mashriq'ul-Adhkár will generate this spiritual energy and channel it for the well-being of the community at large.

Shoghi Effendi in one of his communications referred to the

forces that the American House of Worship, 'this mighty symbol of our Faith', was 'fast releasing in [the] heart of a sorely tried continent'.[24] Systematic and sustained effort in teaching is required for the forces released by the House of Worship to be utilized in worthy and effective ways. He further states that the 'completion of the Temple should . . . release tremendous and unprecedented forces of spiritual energy, destined to be wholly consecrated to the teaching tasks'.[25] The 'creative energies' unleashed by the completion of a House of Worship are 'incalculable'.[26]

The Houses of Worship are concrete expressions of the power of the Faith, taking unique form upon the diverse continents of the planet. Each one of them, as with the buildings of the administrative arc on Mount Carmel, demonstrates and channels divine energy.

The Development of Capacity in Successive Epochs of the Formative Age

We can see how the Administrative Order, teaching plans and the Houses of Worship crystallize and release an ever-increasing measure of the power of the Faith when we consider the growth of the worldwide Bahá'í community in the successive epochs of the Formative Age. We see the capacities and responsibilities of the Bahá'í community expand in each epoch and how each of these periods has been marked by distinctive features.

The first epoch began with the passing of 'Abdu'l-Bahá and the promulgation of His Will and Testament. In this epoch the structure of the Administrative Order came into being as Local and National Assemblies were elected and the Bahá'í community gained the capacity to organize its activities collectively. During this period of the first Seven Year Plan (1937–44), under the guidance of Shoghi Effendi, the number of Local Spiritual Assemblies grew to 60 and the number of National Spiritual Assemblies grew to five. These achievements coincided with the Centenary of the Declaration of the Báb and the holding of the First All-American Bahá'í Convention. The effort to construct the North American House of Worship in Wilmette, near Chicago, was the motivating force in the formation of the first American National Spiritual Assembly, which was originally called the Bahá'í Temple Unity.

In the second epoch of the Formative Age (1944/46–63), these newly created institutions, these incarnations of divine energy, were used to propagate the Faith worldwide. This epoch began with the national teaching plans undertaken by various communities in the 1940s and it culminated in the Ten Year Crusade (1953–63). During this historic period, the number of Local Spiritual Assemblies grew to five thousand, 350 of which were legally incorporated, and the number of National Spiritual Assemblies expanded to 56, with 33 of them incorporated, creating a network covering all the regions of the world where teaching the Faith was allowed. The Houses of Worship in Wilmette, Illinois in the United States and in Kampala, Uganda were completed during this period and the House of Worship in Germany was nearly finished. At the World Centre of the Faith the superstructure of the Shrine of the Báb was erected and the International Archives building was completed.

The third epoch of this transitional period extends from 1963 to 1986 and began with the first election of the Universal House of Justice. During this epoch the world-embracing system that had been established in the World Crusade was strengthened and reinforced. The large regional Assemblies in Africa and the Pacific gave birth to separate National Spiritual Assemblies whose jurisdictions matched those of individual countries. The number of National Spiritual Assemblies grew from 56 in 1963 to 148 in 1986, with a corresponding increase in the number of Local Spiritual Assemblies. The diversity of the Bahá'í community was augmented through the widespread teaching of indigenous peoples. The maturity of Bahá'í communities developed through publications, study programmes and schools. In its message initiating the first teaching plan of the third epoch, the Universal House of Justice set the agenda for the Bahá'í community, 'It must now grow rapidly in size, increase its spiritual cohesion and executive ability, develop its institutions, and extend its influence into all strata of society.'[27] The construction of Bahá'í Houses of Worship in Panama and in India contributed to these processes. The establishment in 1983 of the permanent seat of the Universal House of Justice on the slope of Mount Carmel was a potent symbol of the growing power of the Faith and of its emergence from obscurity on the world stage. It was 'the crowning event' of this period.[28]

The fourth epoch of the Formative Age began in 1986, when the Universal House of Justice devolved onto National Spiritual Assemblies the responsibility of formulating their own goals for the Six Year Plan, which began at Riḍván of that year. The institutions of the Faith had matured during the third epoch of the Formative Age; National and Local Assemblies had learned to interact with government authorities and with the media in their efforts to seek assistance to protect the persecuted believers in Iran; they had tested new teaching methods and made efforts aimed at consolidating Bahá'í community life. They were ready for the next stage of their development – to direct their energies and healing capacities more closely to the needs of all humanity. This new agenda had been foreshadowed by the Universal House of Justice in its Riḍván message of 1983: 'A wider horizon is opening before us, illumined by a growing and universal manifestation of the inherent potentialities of the Cause for ordering human affairs. In this light can be discerned not only our immediate tasks but, more dimly, new pursuits and undertakings upon which we must shortly become engaged' and it outlined these 'oncoming challenges of assisting, as maturity and resources allow, the development of the social and economic life of peoples, of collaborating with the forces leading towards the establishment of order in the world, of influencing the exploitation and constructive uses of modern technology, and in all these ways enhancing the prestige and progress of the Faith and uplifting the conditions of the generality of mankind'.[29]

The worldwide implementation of a well-defined growth process drew the Bahá'í world into the fifth epoch in January 2001, when the Universal House of Justice observed a wholly new level of serious and centred consultation at a gathering of the Counsellors at the World Centre. This further stage in advancing the process of entry by troops has been characterized by a well-focused institute process that has created a common vision, generating excitement about possibilities and emerging successes in drawing increasing numbers of people into the Bahá'í community. Unity of thought, focused action and comprehensive, systematic planning that encompasses the entire planet began to characterize the growth of the Faith.

In the first epoch of the Formative Age we developed the institutions that allow spiritual principles to operate in the lives of humanity. In the second epoch these instruments were erected all over the world. In the third epoch, they were greatly strengthened. In the fourth epoch we began to utilize them with a more outward-facing orientation. The new task of the fifth epoch is to cover the planet systematically with agencies to sustain and accelerate the growth of the Cause.

In this chapter we have seen that spiritual forces are released gradually and that the stages of this process are the stages of the development of the Faith. The crystallization of spiritual forces into the institutions of the Administrative Order, the Houses of Worship and instrumentalities such as systematic plans for teaching, continue to generate creative energies which enable us to resuscitate human souls and build a new civilization. They are the tools God has given us; the concrete embodiment of His purpose for humanity. They have 'irresistible and mysterious power',[30] a 'society-building power',[31] and through them will be created the means by which humanity can attain its destiny.

5

Universal Fermentation and the Impact of Creative Forces on Human Society

Though the wonders of My mercy have encompassed all created things, both visible and invisible, and though the revelations of My grace and bounty have permeated every atom of the universe, yet the rod with which I can chastise the wicked is grievous, and the fierceness of Mine anger against them terrible. *Bahá'u'lláh*[1]

The spiritual forces released by the twin Revelations have created a ferment in human society. Their impact has deranged the world's equilibrium, and this turmoil will continue until humanity conforms itself to God's purpose. We have already seen how spiritual forces originate in the primal will of God, how the Manifestation of God Himself is affected by the tremendous impact of the Revelation reverberating in His soul and how He becomes the instrument through which this energy is released into the world. We have considered how these creative energies take effect, how they are crystallizing into institutions, attitudes and patterns of behaviour which express God's bidding. We have seen how these energies vitalize those who become instruments for the expression of God's will in creation and we have considered the steady unfoldment of the Administrative Order that embodies that force. In this chapter we look at the impact of spiritual forces on whole human societies. The words of the Manifestation of God revolutionize the world through their creative power; they require a response, and humanity's current suffering results from its failure to respond to Bahá'u'lláh's call.

The World is Revolutionized

The immediate and instantaneous effect of divine revelation is renewal and transformation at every level of creation. It has an influence on every person, every entity and every human institution. Spiritual activities transcend space and time; the power of the Word of God is potentially present in every heart. Its force, according to the Báb, is 'vibrating in the innermost realities of all created things'.[2] Bahá'u'lláh Himself writes in a prayer: 'no sooner had the First Word proceeded, through the potency of Thy will and purpose, out of His mouth, and the First Call gone forth from His lips than the whole creation was revolutionized, and all that are in the heavens and all that are on earth were stirred to the depths.' He continues, 'Through that Word the realities of all created things were shaken, were divided, separated, scattered, combined and reunited, disclosing, in both the contingent world and the heavenly kingdom, entities of a new creation . . .'[3]

The world may appear unchanged but it is not. All things are subject to dissolution, change and renovation. New standards, new institutions and new patterns of human interaction have been created and the old ones have lost much of their usefulness and capacity. The world has been recreated in the realm of the spirit; the old forms and structures no longer have validity. No nation is now able to cope on its own with the numerous critical problems that overleap national borders. Ecclesiastical authorities can no longer demand absolute obedience. Bahá'u'lláh has replaced that social bond. It does not work for interest groups to be isolated or for particular classes to work for their own narrow economic interests. Bahá'u'lláh requires love and interdependence among members of the global family. Conforming to the new standards and patterns that the Word of God has decreed for this age brings vitality and joy. Any other pattern of behaviour is empty and deadening.

The unfoldment of civilization is not an arena in which the free will of human beings is fully effective. Bahá'u'lláh admonishes, 'Dost thou believe thou hast the power to frustrate His Will, to hinder Him from executing His judgement, or to deter Him from exercising His sovereignty? Pretendest thou that aught in the heavens or in the earth can resist His Faith? No, by Him Who is the Eternal Truth! Nothing whatsoever in the whole of creation can thwart His Purpose.'[4] If we choose to follow the will of God our actions have meaning and power. If we reject or turn against the will of God for this age, our actions become ineffectual and self-destructive.

The dramatic, sometimes violent, collapse of the old forms and institutions of society demonstrates the disintegrative force at work in the world, a part of what Shoghi Effendi calls the major plan of God. A 'God-born Force, irresistible in its sweeping power, incalculable in its potency', has sundered 'the age-old ties which for centuries have held together the fabric of civilized society'.[5] He calls it 'a great and mighty wind of God' and describes it as 'invading the remotest and fairest regions of the earth, rocking its foundations, deranging its equilibrium, sundering its nations, disrupting the homes of its peoples, wasting its cities, driving into exile its kings, pulling down its bulwarks, uprooting its institutions, dimming its light, and harrowing up the souls of its inhabitants'. He also refers to it as a 'cleansing force' and says that it will be 'unimaginably glorious in its ultimate consequences'.[6] The wind of God blows away the rigid, worn out, lifeless structures and institutions of society so that new ones more appropriate to the time can arise.

A Time of Painful Transition

We live in a violent, confused and tumultuous world. This is a time of far-reaching transition. The crisis of our era, in the words of Shoghi Effendi, is 'incomprehensible to man, and admittedly unprecedented in the annals of the human race'.[7] But chaos has become the norm for the generations that have grown up since the coming of Bahá'u'lláh. Shoghi Effendi describes the process of change through which humanity is collectively passing, writing that the Faith of Bahá'u'lláh 'has, through the emergence of its slowly-crystallizing system, induced a fermentation in the general life of mankind designed to shake the very foundations of a disordered society, to purify its life-blood, to reorientate and reconstruct its institutions, and shape its final destiny'.[8]

This societal fermentation is a painful, disorderly, disturbing transition from old to new, from a lower condition to a higher one. A substance undergoing fermentation is agitated and unsettled, elements within it are broken apart, gradually reorganized and transformed into something entirely new by the process.

Another way to understand the impact of divine revelation on society is to think of the birthing process. Bahá'u'lláh uses the word 'travail', meaning pain, anguish or suffering, specifically from childbirth, to describe humanity's condition. Shoghi Effendi later refers to 'the birth of the Order now stirring in the womb of a travailing age'.[9] He enumerates some of the profound changes that are taking place and explains that they are evidence of the pain of a society that is in labour and that persists in ignoring Bahá'u'lláh's call.

> In the convulsions of contemporary society, in the frenzied, world-wide ebullitions of men's thoughts, in the fierce antagonisms inflaming races, creeds and classes, in the shipwreck of nations, in the downfall of kings, in the dismemberment of empires, in the extinction of dynasties, in the collapse of ecclesiastical hierarchies, in the deterioration of time-honoured institutions, in the dissolution of ties, secular as well as religious, that had for so long held together the members of the human race . . . in these we can readily recognize the evidences of the travail of an age that has sustained the impact of His Revelation, that has ignored His summons, and is now labouring to be delivered of its burden, as a direct consequence of the impulse communicated to it by the generative, the purifying, the transmuting influence of His Spirit.[10]

Bahá'u'lláh has cast the seed of a new world civilization, metaphorically speaking, into the womb of global human consciousness, and humanity, for its part, has to nurture, develop and give birth to His World Order. If society had recognized Bahá'u'lláh's Revelation when it was given, that process would have been very much simpler. Childbirth is smoother when the mother is alert, accepting and participating in the process; if she fights the birth, then her physical difficulty and pain increase.

Why Humanity is Suffering

Ignorance of the role of Bahá'u'lláh and the rejection of His World Order are the principal causes of humanity's current pain. Shoghi Effendi, whose keen assessment of world conditions is still so apt today, writes, 'The whole of mankind is groaning, is dying to be led to unity, and to terminate its age-long martyrdom. And yet it stubbornly refuses to embrace the light and acknowledge the sovereign authority of the one Power that can extricate it from its entanglements, and avert the woeful calamity that threatens to engulf it.'[11] Moreover, 'the fires lit by this great ordeal are the consequence of men's failure to recognize' the 'vast process now operating in the world' through the Revelation of Bahá'u'lláh.[12]

Humanity has repeatedly been given the opportunity to hear the divine summons, first by the Manifestation of God Himself. Bahá'u'lláh directly addressed the most powerful among the civil and religious leaders of the day with His resounding call. As 'Abdu'l-Bahá points out:

> Bahá'u'lláh declared the Most Great Peace and international arbitration. He voiced these principles in numerous Epistles which were circulated broadcast throughout the East. He wrote to all the kings and rulers, encouraging, advising and admonishing them in regard to the establishment of peace, making it evident by conclusive proofs that the happiness and glory of humanity can only be assured through disarmament and arbitration.[13]

And Shoghi Effendi outlines in somewhat greater detail:

> . . . Bahá'u'lláh . . . proclaimed His Message to the kings and rulers of both the East and the West, both Christian and Muslim, addressed the Pope, the Caliph of Islám, the Chief Magistrates of the Republics of the American continent, the entire Christian sacerdotal order, the leaders of Shí'ih and Sunní Islám, and the high priests of the Zoroastrian religion.[14]

The Guardian characterizes the deplorable response of those who, at that time, were informed of Bahá'u'lláh's claim:

> Unmitigated indifference on the part of men of eminence and
> rank; unrelenting hatred shown by the ecclesiastical dignitaries
> of the Faith from which it had sprung; the scornful derision of
> the people among whom it was born; the utter contempt which
> most of those kings and rulers who had been addressed by its
> Author manifested towards it . . . the distortion to which its prin-
> ciples and laws were subjected by the envious and the malicious,
> in lands and among peoples far beyond the country of its origin
> – all these are but the evidences of the treatment meted out by a
> generation sunk in self-content, careless of its God, and oblivious
> of the omens, prophecies, warnings and admonitions revealed by
> His Messengers.[15]

Following on with this theme, the Guardian implies that the 'inter-
mittent crises' that we see convulsing global society are:

> . . . due primarily to the lamentable inability of the world's recog-
> nized leaders to read aright the signs of the times, to rid themselves
> once for all of their preconceived ideas and fettering creeds, and
> to reshape the machinery of their respective governments accord-
> ing to those standards that are implicit in Bahá'u'lláh's supreme
> declaration of the Oneness of Mankind.[16]

Under the guidance of the Universal House of Justice, efforts to
awaken world leaders and humankind at large have continued.
In 1967 the representatives of mankind were again informed of
Bahá'u'lláh's message when 140 of the world's Heads of State were
officially presented with a volume of His writings. Many expressed
appreciation of the teachings but very few followed up in any
meaningful way and only one formally embraced Bahá'u'lláh's
Cause. In 2002 Bahá'ís around the world approached heads of
various faith groups to deliver the message of the Universal House
of Justice to the world's religious leaders. The Bahá'í International
Community has presented numerous statements relating to various aspects of Bahá'u'lláh's message to dignitaries, like-minded

organizations, United Nations committees and even to delegates of the Millennium World Peace Summit held in New York in August 2000. Significant worldwide effort has also been made to acquaint the public with the Bahá'í teachings directly, through the media and by setting up informational websites.

Only when people learn what Bahá'u'lláh expects of them and put it into action will their afflictions be alleviated.

Active resistance to Bahá'u'lláh is another reason for the violence and turmoil of this period of transition. It is not just the effect of the Revelation in the world that is producing this chaos but the fact that a significant part of humanity has consciously resisted it. When Bahá'u'lláh offered the Most Great Peace to the kings and rulers of the earth in their representation of all mankind, His call went unheeded. This prompted Him to declare that sovereignty would be removed from the empires and dynasties of kings and given into the hands of the people. In 1953 Shoghi Effendi published a chronology of the events related to Bahá'u'lláh's proclamation to the kings, which listed the extinction of monarchy after monarchy, year after year.[17] Some 40 more have fallen since 1953. Whoever or whatever institution resists the plan of God will forfeit its power. Such has been the fate of empires and kings and of formerly all-powerful ecclesiastical institutions of various religions. The age-old social, intellectual, political and economic ties that had bound the world together in firm ways have been broken, thus allowing society to realign itself in new patterns consonant with Bahá'u'lláh's proclamation of the oneness and wholeness of the human race.

Humanity's suffering is not only an inevitable consequence of rejecting Bahá'u'lláh, and a punishment for that failing, it is also the means that serves to purify and unify the human race. Shoghi Effendi describes the world's current crisis as an all-consuming fire but not one that burns until nothing is left. It is a cleansing and galvanizing fire that melts strong, resistant elements and blends them together. As he explains, 'nothing short of the fire of a severe ordeal, unparalleled in its intensity, can fuse and weld the discordant entities that constitute the elements of present-day civilization, into the integral components of the world commonwealth of the future'.[18] He described the titanic upheaval of World War II as:

. . . a direct interposition by Him Who is the Ordainer of the Universe, the Judge of all men, and the Deliverer of the nations. It is the rod of both the anger of God and of His correction. The fierceness of its devastating power chastens the children of men for their refusal to acclaim the century-old Message of their promised, their Heaven-sent Redeemer. The fury of its flames, on the other hand, purges away the dross, and welds the limbs of humanity into one single organism, indivisible, purified, God-conscious and Divinely directed.[19]

The world we live in is turbulent and chaotic because it is changing from one state of being to another. Under the impact of the Word of God, human society is in ferment. It is giving birth to a new social order. The suffering that humanity is enduring in this period of transition, though not of His choosing, is now an inescapable factor in the healing plan of God. Things could have been very different if the representatives of mankind who received the original summons of Bahá'u'lláh had recognized His divine mission and implemented His plan for the benefit of all but that opportunity was tragically missed. Now the only way forward leads through the widespread pain and disruption which is so clear around us. We can take comfort in the knowledge that this suffering will help people to learn to distinguish between poison and honey, between fire and light, to discern between the stone and the pearl, between illusion and reality, and move society to develop the spiritual powers that Bahá'u'lláh intends for us.

Acting on an Understanding of the State of the World

As conditions worsen we can read in the evidences of the breakdown of the world signs of the unfoldment of this destined course leading toward the new dawn that God has immutably fixed for humanity. In other words, we should be motivated and energized by witnessing what is happening in the world. We should try to see with the eye of God, as He asks us to do. God sees the present world as 'spiritually destitute, morally bankrupt, politically disrupted, socially convulsed, economically paralysed, writhing, bleeding and breaking up',[20] about to give way to a new order. It is coming apart so that the various elements can be put back together in an infinitely superior way. If a building that was once strong and useful has become irreparably run down and dangerously dilapidated, residents of the area understand that the dust and noise of demolition, while unpleasant, are signs of improvement and harbingers of renewal. Likewise, the expert gardener, seeing that an old and ailing rosebush has been severely cut back in the winter and suddenly deprived of a large part of its living substance, understands that this drastic event will give it the best possible chance for healthy regrowth in the spring. There are many such parallels in nature and in society. It is always somewhat unsettling, at a minimum, to lose the familiar but renewal and growth do not take place without change.

In today's landscape of transition we are assailed by wrenching images of people fleeing violence, children separated from their parents and loved ones dying. We cannot help but perceive and be touched by the pain, sorrow, anxiety and fear all about us but must strive to see the tumult of the world through God's vision instead of our own. This will give us courage and power. God, with the perspective that allows Him to see both the beginning and the end of things, observes the world in a purifying process that will lead to a higher, more merciful stage of civilization.

On the international stage over the past century, one world war motivated peoples to form the League of Nations but that attempt was not sufficiently inclusive and lacked vigour. The next world war precipitated the formation of the United Nations but its creators held back from giving it the requisite authority. Humanity has not yet approached the problem of global governance by drawing on that spiritual energy which is the source of well-being in human affairs. Seeing with the eye of God gives us the capacity to acknowledge and confront the problems around us, and compels us to work towards the recognition by humanity that this suffering can only be alleviated through the universal application of the spirit and form of Bahá'u'lláh's remedy.

Those who see only with limited human vision can become depressed and paralysed by the circumstances of the world. The situation is so overwhelming that much of humanity flees from a sense of responsibility through relentless pursuit of crass materialism, trivial distractions or alcohol and drugs. We, as believers in Bahá'u'lláh's message, on the other hand, know that humanity's suffering has a purpose. The human race will not be obliterated. The pain and distress of innocents in this world is amply recompensed in the next. Peace is not only possible but inevitable. We do not despair of the present because Bahá'u'lláh's Revelation gives us a vision of the future.

Understanding the role of God in human affairs, however, does not give Bahá'ís permission to become complacent and leave the world's problems for Him to solve miraculously on His own. On the contrary, we are exhorted to be 'anxiously concerned with the needs of the age ye live in, and centre your deliberations on its exigencies and requirements'[21] and to 'turn [our] faces from the darkness of estrangement to the effulgent light of the daystar of unity.'[22] In His Most Holy Book, Bahá'u'lláh calls upon us to 'assist' God 'with works of righteousness, and also through wisdom and utterance.'[23] We cannot think that all we have to do is wait until catastrophe strikes and then go sweep up afterwards. We are responsible, as the bearers of the Word of God in this Day, to exert ourselves to the utmost both to shorten this painful period in history by ensuring that Bahá'u'lláh's Revelation is understood and to assuage human suffering to the extent possible. As the Universal House of Justice said in a sobering message dated October 1967, 'Upon our efforts depends in very large measure the fate of humanity.'[24]

All the activities of the Bahá'í community are, at a profound level, its response to the suffering that humanity experiences because of its indifference to God's message for this day. We engage in a culture of systematic learning about the Revelation so that we can equip ourselves to serve Bahá'u'lláh and move society closer to Him. We offer children's classes and youth activities to orient young people in the same direction. Devotional gatherings give us spiritual strength and enhance our ability to see the workings of the world as they really are. These systematic activities enable us to engage the general public with the authority, beauty, power and dynamism of the Bahá'í writings. When people around the world understand and implement the teachings, their agony will end.

The Inner and Outer Dimensions of the Plan of God Converge

The forces of integration and the forces of disintegration are both intensifying. This was pointed out by the Universal House of Justice in the aforementioned message of October 1967: 'the struggle between the forces of darkness – man's lower nature – and the rising sun of the Divine teachings which draw him on to his true station, intensifies day by day'.[25] The driving power of the catastrophic tempest sweeping the face of the earth 'is remorselessly gaining in range and momentum'[26] but, at the same time, the constructive forces operating in the world are concentrated in what Shoghi Effendi called the minor plan of God and are becoming stronger. National and Local Spiritual Assemblies in every part of the world are developing their understanding of Bahá'u'lláh's Revelation, they practise the skill of consultation and are increasingly demonstrating their ability to apply Bahá'í principles to solve the problems people face. The institute process allows individuals and communities to move coherently and efficiently towards higher levels of capacity. The mapping of clusters facilitates well-ordered growth in the present and will facilitate Bahá'í engagement with the needs of the greater society in the future.

As the Bahá'í Order becomes stronger and the world around it falls apart, the integrative and the disintegrative forces of God's plan for humanity will continue to interact. Surely the time will come when communities, social agencies and nations themselves, unable to bear the pain of their failures any longer, will increasingly turn to the Bahá'í plan and its institutions for guidance and support. These institutions, 'the one refuge within which a sore-tried humanity, purged from its dross, can attain its destiny',[27] will then progressively achieve their capacity for the enlightenment and well-being of the human race. This convergence will mark the beginning of a new phase in history, in which the spiritual forces released by Bahá'u'lláh will find ever greater expression in the organization of human affairs.

Crisis and Victory

Progress towards the goal of the unification and spiritualization of the entire family of man does not take place in a smooth and linear manner. Energy, both earthly and spiritual, is characterized by cycles, and forward movement takes place through accelerations and setbacks. Looking back on the history of the Faith, this pattern of pulsations is unmistakable. The Guardian outlines it for us in a number of places, including the final paragraphs of *God Passes By*, his masterful account of the history of the first hundred years of the Bahá'í dispensation. In those concluding paragraphs he summarizes the long succession of events, from the Declaration of the Báb and the 'outburst of savage fanaticism' that greeted it, through a progression of triumphs and crises, culminating in a series of outstanding developments in the early and mid-20th century – the liberation of the Holy Land, the World Centre of our Faith, from Ottoman rule; the failure of carefully laid plans of ill-wishers of the Cause; the widening growth of the Bahá'í community across the globe; and the achievement of various forms of public recognition of the Faith, obtained from a number of religious and civil authorities of the day, including the Council of the League of Nations.

The crises that have had a major impact on the development of the Faith have usually taken the form of attacks – external, from those who wield temporal or spiritual authority, or internal, from self-seeking, ambitious individuals. The striking thing about all these assaults is that, instead of harming the Cause of God, they serve as fuel to propel it forward.

'Abdu'l-Bahá assures us that oppression serves as 'the wind that doth fan the fire of the Love of God'[28] and advises the believers to welcome persecution, for it acts, however unwittingly, as an agent of the forces of light. He pointed out how the enemies of the Faith have unintentionally helped its development from the very beginning by directing the attention of the public towards it, thus publicizing the teachings far and wide, and says that Bahá'u'lláh pronounced the antagonistic members of the clergy 'the couriers of the Cause'.[29]

The Guardian characterizes the various kinds of attacks and persecutions as 'the life-blood' of the institutions of the Faith, and 'an inseparable and intrinsic part of its development and growth.'[30] He makes it clear that 'opposition to the Faith' is the 'motive-power' that 'galvanizes' the 'souls of its valiant defenders' and 'taps for them' 'fresh springs' of 'Divine and inexhaustible Energy.'[31]

In a defining passage Shoghi Effendi explains that the forward movement of the Faith 'propelled by the stimulating influences which the unwisdom of its enemies and the force latent within itself both engender, resolves itself into a series of rhythmic pulsations, precipitated, on the one hand, through the explosive outbursts of its foes, and the vibrations of Divine Power, on the other, which speed it, with ever-increasing momentum, along that predestined course traced for it by the Hand of the Almighty.'[32]

While the Bahá'í spirit requires us to use wisdom and to avoid argument and conflict, if persecution nevertheless arises we are urged to face it in a positive frame of mind. The Guardian advised that:

> The friends should . . . not assume an attitude of mere resignation in the face of persecutions. They should rather welcome them, and utilize them as means for their own spiritual uplift and also for the promotion of the Cause. As the Faith grows stronger and attracts the serious attention and consideration of the world outside, the friends must expect [an] . . . increase in the forces of opposition which from every direction, both secular and religious, will be massed to undermine the very basis of its existence. The final outcome of such a struggle, which will be surely gigantic, is clear to us believers. A Faith born of God and guided by His Divine and all-pervasive spirit cannot but finally triumph and firmly establish itself, no matter how persistent and insidious the forces with which it has to contend. The friends should be confident, and act with the utmost wisdom and moderation, and should particularly abstain from any provocative act. The future is surely theirs.[33]

It is evident that crises can be very painful and can often cause temporary setbacks but that the Faith always emerges triumphant

and purified. The attitude with which believers should face opposition is also clear. 'Abdu'l-Bahá's counsel remains:

> You must withstand them with the utmost love and kindness;
> consider their oppression and persecution as the caprice of chil-
> dren, and do not give any importance to whatever they do. For
> at the end the illumination of the Kingdom will overwhelm the
> darkness of the world . . . Rest ye assured.[34]

Crises provide fresh fuel for the Cause to go forward. They are,
in a sense, a reward for preceding hard-won victories and they
engender, in their turn, further triumphs. The Guardian explains
the process in saying that:

> . . . the mere progress of the Cause by provoking the hatreds and
> jealousies of peoples and nations, creates for itself such difficulties
> and obstacles as only its divine spirit can overcome. 'Abdu'l-Bahá
> has emphatically stated that the enmity and opposition of the
> world will increase in direct proportion to the extension and
> progress of [the] Faith. The greater the zeal of the believers and
> the more striking the effect of their achievements, the fiercer will
> be the opposition of the enemy.
>   . . . But side by side with such emphatic predictions is the
> assurance that out of these sufferings and trials His Cause will
> emerge triumphant and purified.[35]

From all these statements we understand that the Cause of God
need not fear opposition. Far from it, as history has proved.
Though the unfoldment of the Faith of Bahá'u'lláh has been
attended by trials even more severe than those experienced by
past religions, we see that – in contrast with the previous religions
– these ordeals have not only failed to rupture its unity but have
been unable to produce even a temporary split in the community.
Instead, the ranks of the believers are strengthened by such trials,
being 'under the protection of the resistless power and inscrutable
providence of God'.[36]

In this chapter we have examined the impact of the creative

energies of Bahá'u'lláh's Revelation on the world as a whole. Turmoil on every level of society is the consequence of old social forms resisting a God-ordained change, losing their power and effectiveness as the world struggles to give birth to a new society. A new world will come into existence through the pulsations of a succession of crises and victories, having been shaped by new standards, new institutions and new principles revealed by Bahá'u'lláh. Bahá'í institutions, the outer incarnation of God's unseen purpose, bear a tremendous responsibility to demonstrate to humanity the way forward.

6

Understanding Forces of Darkness

Methinks people's sense of taste hath, alas, been sorely affected by
the fever of negligence and folly, for they are found to be wholly
unconscious and deprived of the sweetness of His utterance.
Bahá'u'lláh[1]

The human race, in its rejection of Bahá'u'lláh, has turned away
from God. This has, in consequence, brought about a surge of
dark and destructive forces. These forces are not psychic or super-
natural; they are the negative qualities, beliefs and tendencies that
human beings manifest when they deny their spiritual nature.
They arise from man's lower animal aspect, and they impact not
only individuals but whole societies.

It could seem superfluous or unbecoming to study the forces
of darkness at work in the world in the face of the tremendous and
overwhelming forces of light revealed by Bahá'u'lláh. However,
Shoghi Effendi urges Bahá'ís to 'open their eyes to the existing
conditions, study the evil forces that are at play and then with a
concerted effort arise and bring about the necessary reforms'.[2]
Understanding the operation of dark forces is an essential step in
creating a new civilization, as it will help us greatly in keeping to
the path of light. Through a fearless look at the forces of darkness operating both within and around us we become empowered.
'Abdu'l-Bahá wrote that 'truthfulness is the foundation of all the
virtues of the world of humanity' and that 'without truthfulness,
progress and success in all of the worlds of God are impossible for
a soul'.[3] If we are not truthful with ourselves, if we do not acknowl-

edge how we are affected by negative forces, how then will we counteract them?

In this chapter we explore the way in which dark forces emerge and examine how Shoghi Effendi has defined them. We will find irreligion and materialism as the root of all such forces and will then look at the powerful influence they currently have on the societies in which we live. Chapter 7 offers insight into how we can combat these forces of darkness.

The Dual Nature of Human Beings

The Bahá'í writings attribute two natures to human beings – a spiritual nature and an animal or lower nature. The physical body – the animal nature – is the means through which human beings exist in this physical plane. A person's true and eternal reality, however, is the human spirit. Our physical being operates in accordance with the laws of the animal kingdom, and the lower aspect of a person is intended to become the servant of the higher, spiritual nature. The human body may be compared to a horse and the human spirit to its rider. When the rider is in control, the horse becomes a very useful vehicle that can scale mountains, undertake difficult journeys and accomplish what the human spirit aspires to do. If the rider is not in control of the horse, the animal nature of the person will dominate the spiritual aspect and the horse then takes the rider wherever it desires. Driven by self and passion, the horse constantly endangers both the equilibrium and the well-being of the rider.

Dark forces emerge when the lower, animal nature of human beings becomes dominant. The force of the animal nature is self-centred; it motivates people to act in selfish ways. Deception, aggression, competition and sheltering within the herd are survival strategies for animals but the human spirit is endowed with the capacity to manifest honesty, selflessness and altruistic love. When individuals are violent, self-seeking, cowardly or indolent they are being ruled by their animal nature.

According to the Bahá'í teachings, there is no single, independent evil power in the world. The Devil, or the 'Evil One', is any human being while in submission to his or her base animal nature. All of the talents of human beings – our intellectual vision and creative capacities – can be diverted and perverted by our lower nature into very real and powerful negative forces.

God has left choice open to us but the whole longing and purpose of the Divine Educators is to lift man out of inertia, ignorance, selfishness and complacency, to inspire each individual to attune his heart to God's will, learn to subdue the lower self and rise to the joyous, empowered and exalted condition for which he was created.

> Man has the power both to do good and to do evil; if his power for good predominates and his inclinations to do wrong are conquered, then man in truth may be called a saint. But if, on the contrary, he rejects the things of God and allows his evil passions to conquer him, then he is no better than a mere animal.
>
> Saints are men who have freed themselves from the world of matter and who have overcome sin. They live in the world but are not of it, their thoughts being continually in the world of the spirit. Their lives are spent in holiness, and their deeds show forth love, justice and godliness.[4]

The exaltation by man's free will of selfish instincts over his spiritual nature, if unchecked, can permeate a whole society with dark forces. Under the influence of social movements that appeal to human fears and insecurities, people can be led to behave in ways that are at once selfish, violent and reactive. Egotistical religious leaders from a wide variety of denominations, obsessed with preserving their own status, have often fostered superstition, fanaticism and narrow orthodoxy in the hearts and minds of their followers, at times leading even to bloodshed against the 'other'. Self-seeking demagogues preaching doctrines of ethnic and racial superiority have infected populations, caused enormous suffering, instigated massacres and have even led to genocide. However large and impersonal these dark forces in society may become, they have derived in the first place from the lower nature of individual human beings. People make the choices that lead to evil in the world: there is no external source called Satan where blame can be placed.

Good and evil, paradise and hell, are the outcome of our choices, and 'Abdu'l-Bahá points out that 'the paradise and hell of existence are found in all the worlds of God, whether in this world or in the spiritual heavenly worlds'.[5] Bahá'u'lláh clarifies this when He says, of paradise and hell, that, 'The one is reunion with Me; the other thine own self'.[6] And again: 'Every good thing is of God, and every evil thing is from yourselves'.[7]

Consequences of the Individual's Choice

It is not possible for humanity to avoid or ignore the Word of God. Neither is it possible for the individual, once aware of Bahá'u'lláh's claim, to sidestep it. Bahá'u'lláh asserts that, 'No sooner had that Revelation been unveiled to men's eyes than the signs of universal discord appeared among the peoples of the world, and commotion seized the dwellers of earth and heaven, and the foundations of all things were shaken'.[8] He relates that when the forces of dissension were released, everything acquired a distinct and individual character; the fires of Hell blazed and the delights of Paradise were uncovered. He further affirms that whoever turns towards God is blessed and whoever denies Him is beset by woe. This is a very mysterious passage but one understanding that we get from it is that every soul ultimately takes a position in relation to the Revelation. Each can become, will become, either aligned with the forces of good or overshadowed by forces of evil. Until, through the exercise of his own free will, the individual takes a positive stand and embraces the forces of light, he leaves himself open to forces of darkness, even without having made a conscious choice to do so.

When speaking of forces of evil, it is important to recall that the Bahá'í teachings maintain that evil is not a thing of itself but rather simply a lack of good. 'Abdu'l-Bahá explains that:

> . . . evil is nothingness; so death is the absence of life. When man no longer receives life, he dies. Darkness is the absence of light:

when there is no light, there is darkness. Light is an existing thing, but darkness is nonexistent. Wealth is an existing thing, but poverty is nonexisting.

Then it is evident that all evils return to nonexistence. Good exists; evil is nonexistent.[9]

The fact that evil is essentially only the absence of good does not mean that it is not a factor to be reckoned with in the world. If we imagine a human being who is fundamentally devoid of good qualities – from whom there is no show of kindness, no love; no honesty, generosity, respectfulness, truthfulness; no trustworthiness, no compassion – we understand that the actions of such a person will necessarily be detrimental to others and to himself. Those acts would commonly be thought of as bad, ungodly or evil. In an individual inclined in this negative direction, the greater his natural vigour, the more harm can be done to those around him and to society. The life energy of every person comes from God but the choice of how to use it is left to each human soul. 'Abdu'l-Bahá's brief explanation is key:

> . . . the inaction or the movement of man depend upon the assistance of God. If he is not aided, he is not able to do either good or evil. But when the help of existence comes from the Generous Lord, he is able to do both good and evil; but if the help is cut off, he remains absolutely helpless . . . So this condition is like that of a ship which is moved by the power of the wind or steam; if this power ceases, the ship cannot move at all. Nevertheless, the rudder of the ship turns it to either side, and the power of the steam moves it in the desired direction. If it is directed to the east, it goes to the east; or if it is directed to the west, it goes to the west. This motion does not come from the ship; no, it comes from the wind or the steam.
>
> In the same way, in all the action or inaction of man, he receives power from the help of God; but the choice of good or evil belongs to the man himself.[10]

The Revelation transforms all things. We have already discussed what changes occur within those souls who align themselves with it. The souls who resist the Word of God are also changed; they play a different kind of role, however. Resistance is a matter of degree but it is clear that a negative force derives from the individuals that deliberately oppose the Revelation, that react against it. To the degree that they oppose God's will, they become contributors to chaos in the world. A soul that chooses to be separate from the organic structure through which flows the new energy that has been breathed into humanity cuts itself off from the higher life force of the spirit. If such a condition persists, it seems as though a kind of withering takes place – like that of a yellowing leaf barely attached to the tree or an arm deprived of essential connection to the nervous system – and the individual can become almost a shadow of itself, a human form bereft of spiritual vitality. The ability to make healthy contributions to the development of society is then constrained and the capacity to sustain appropriate human relationships is diminished. When such ailing souls are numerous, their malfunction and deterioration become apparent in the breakdown of the social order.

Of course the response to the divine summons on the part of an individual soul is not always immediate acceptance or rejection. Often there is a period of hesitation or perplexity – and each of us remains free at every moment, as we make the endless major and minor decisions of life, to turn towards what God asks of us or to turn away.

Identifying Dark Forces

In his writings Shoghi Effendi refers to and describes many specific forces of darkness. Paying close attention to such references helps us to base our thinking about reality on a spiritual foundation. Among the forces of darkness identified by the Guardian are conditions that appear in humanity when it turns away from God: irreligion, atheism, naturalism, unbelief, secularism and paganism. Other dark forces named by Shoghi Effendi are what a wayward humanity worships in place of God: materialism, nationalism, racialism and communism. He conveys the perversions of religion with another set of terms, among them being fanaticism and superstition. Still other dark forces are the consequences of humanity's losing the moral compass provided by living religion: prejudice, corruption, immorality, moral laxity and widespread lawlessness, for example. Dark forces, he likewise states, include elements which accelerate the decline of humanity's fortunes: violence, disorder, rebellion, revolt, anarchy, disunity, inharmony, separation, schism, disintegration, hatred, suspicion, despair, reaction and decay. These are the dark forces, whether they are expressed individually in our lives or collectively in the cultures and societies that surround us. They mislead us and keep us from turning to the world of God.

In vivid contrast are those forces of light mentioned in the Bahá'í sacred writings. These include forces that derive directly from authentic religion: justice, trustworthiness, compassion, faith, interdependence, universality, insight, godliness, wisdom, rectitude, holiness and peace. Of course all of these overlap but we can see some forces of light particularly as spiritual qualities resulting from our connection to God, such as love, unity, harmony, purity, consideration, courage, courtesy and humility. Others are the outcome of faith and obedience to the divine teachings, such as happiness, detachment, acquiescence, magnanimity, integrity, truthfulness, sagacity, uprightness, moderation, chastity, trust and hope. Yet others are conditions that will heal the world: reconciliation, pacification, integration, orderliness, fellowship, non-violence and freedom from prejudice. This is a partial list, gleaned from the Bahá'í writings; it helps us remember what we have to work with and draw strength from as we confront the forces of darkness.

The Force of Irreligion

A prime force of darkness is irreligion. It robs us of our understanding of the very purpose of life. It gives rise to materialism. It closes the door to the sources of power and well-being for humanity. Irreligion and materialism promote other dark forces. Whenever people lose their authentic religious foundation, their spiritual fibre, there is little left but the physical shell of their beings, their animal selves. Their whole focus becomes the outer, ephemeral benefits of life and how to acquire them: they lose sight of their innate nobility and the heights of spiritual development to which human beings can aspire. This turning away from the higher nature and towards the lower nature spurs the growth of forces of darkness.

Bahá'u'lláh condemned irreligion in the world. His writings demonstrate how the spiritual vitality of earlier religions has been sapped by egotistical leadership and self-serving interpretations, and how a lack of true faith and understanding prevails among the mass of the people. He laments how, because of the false religious standards of the times and the waywardness of the people, there was no ear able to hear His message and no eye able to perceive Him.

It is important to make a distinction between true religion, a living force that connects human hearts with God while bringing light and unity into the world, and what is often taken for religion, consisting mainly of form and ceremony, with much of the original teaching having become misunderstood or lost sight of. This state of affairs has come about in the winter of each cycle of religious renewal.[11] Fanaticism, superstition, priestcraft, orthodoxy, narrowness and sectarian tendencies of whatever denomination are all forces of darkness that have long since lost connection with the spirit of the divine Messengers whom they claim to represent. Faithlessness and godlessness can characterize people who are very involved in practising an imitation of religion. Emphasizing this point in a talk in the West, 'Abdu'l-Bahá described the condition of irreligion:

> . . . they have taken away the heavenly light of divine truth and sit in the darkness of imitations and imaginations. That which was meant to be conducive to life has become the cause of death; that which should have been an evidence of knowledge is now a proof of ignorance; that which was a factor in the sublimity of human nature has proved to be its degradation.[12]

In another of His talks, the Master said that the light of true religion had been extinguished owing to human interpretations and disagreement.[13] What remained of the beauteous and harmonizing civilizing force of past religious dispensations was now an empty shell, an imitation; true religion had been forgotten. It was now just a form, without the essence of religion, which is a unifying, clarifying, mind-awakening, all-encompassing force of love that defines the nature of existence and motivates positive action.

> Inasmuch as human interpretations and blind imitations differ widely, religious strife and disagreement have arisen among mankind, the light of true religion has been extinguished and the unity of the world of humanity destroyed. The Prophets of God voiced the spirit of unity and agreement. They have been the Founders of divine reality. Therefore, if the nations of the world forsake imitations and investigate the reality underlying the revealed Word of God, they will agree and become reconciled.[14]

This is not to say there are no good intentions remaining among the followers of past religions. There appear to be many sincere people in groups of all kinds, both religious and secular; however 'Abdu'l-Bahá explains that in order to produce the desired result, sincere intention needs to be accompanied by volition and action, as well as the requisite knowledge.[15] When the aim is to change attitudes and human behaviour, good intentions need to be supported by clear understanding and connected to a powerful source of dynamic energy capable of generating both volition and action. The Word of God, always divinely tailored for the needs of humankind at its current stage of development, provides that unique motive energy.

> The various sects who today consider themselves servants of the world of humanity are possessed of good intention, but . . . many a good intention was there in the world of existence which left no trace, for it was not confirmed by the effective power. But the good intentions of the . . . friends are enforced by the power of the Word of God; therefore, it is effective and quick in action and the means of life to the world of humanity.[16]

> Today on this earth there are many souls who are the spreaders of
> peace and reconciliation and are longing for the realization of the
> oneness and unity of the world of man; but this intention needs
> a dynamic power, so that it may become manifest in the world of
> being.[17]

Irreligion comes in a variety of forms, one of which has been
termed functional atheism. We see a lot of this in the world
today. A person may think that God exists but believe that human
nature, economic forces or political traditions are the reason that
things are, inevitably, the way they are. Generations of people
have, understandably, failed to find much relevance to what passes
under the name of religion, have come to consider it as a spent
force and have basically adopted a secular, atheistic view of reality.
Their whole tendency is not to believe, or to see God as pertinent
only to the individual and not to society as a whole.

In another context Bahá'u'lláh says that a physical illness can
act as a barrier blocking the sustaining energy that flows from the
soul to the body, like a cloud coming between the sun and the
earth.[18] Irreligion, secularism and the belief that political or economic forces alone animate humanity are spiritual illnesses. They
act as veils or clouds, hindering and delaying the influence and
action of the divine spirit of Bahá'u'lláh in human affairs.

Materialism

In one of His talks 'Abdu'l-Bahá gives a very vivid explanation
about the rise of materialism. After speaking about humankind's
superiority to the material world and praising religion as a path-
way conducive to the progress and upliftment of the world, He
laments the general eclipse of the light of God in society, saying:

> Alas that humanity is completely submerged in imitations and
> unrealities, notwithstanding that the truth of divine religion has
> ever remained the same. Superstitions have obscured the funda-
> mental reality, the world is darkened . . . rites and dogmas are many
> and various; therefore, discord has arisen among the religious

systems, whereas religion is for the unification of mankind. True religion is the source of love and agreement amongst men . . . but the people are holding to the counterfeit and imitation . . . Therefore, the realm of the religionist has gradually narrowed and darkened, and the sphere of the materialist has widened and advanced; for the religionist has held to imitation and counterfeit, neglecting and discarding holiness and the sacred reality of religion. When the sun sets, it is the time for bats to fly. They come forth because they are creatures of the night. When the lights of religion become darkened, the materialists appear. They are the bats of night. The decline of religion is their time of activity; they seek the shadows when the world is darkened and clouds have spread over it.[19]

A great many of the widely-accepted theories and concepts of the world about us are fundamentally materialistic: they have gained popularity because their outlook is confined to man's material existence and usually pander to selfish instincts. Often the appeal is made to one ethnic group, or racial group, or social class, to advance themselves at the expense of others. Sometimes it is just a general appeal to the egotistical tendencies of human beings. This is clearly the case with many ephemeral fads of self-help popular psychology, some groupings generally thought of as religious and, at times, even movements whose stated goal proposes improving the conditions of society. Such schemes and plans for the betterment of the human race attract people for a time but once they are tested their inadequacy becomes evident. They are dissolved, as Shoghi Effendi indicates, by the very forces that had given rise to them. In defining these phenomena he states:

> Springing from a finite mind, begotten of human fancy, and oftentimes the product of ill-conceived designs, such movements succeed, by reason of their novelty, their appeal to man's baser instincts and their dependence upon the resources of a sordid world, in dazzling for a time the eyes of men, only to plunge finally from the heights of their meteoric career into the darkness of oblivion, dissolved by the very forces that had assisted in their creation.[20]

Because of their materialistic perception of reality, communism and capitalism are described as twin sisters. Neither one has created a just and prosperous society. Human beings are fundamentally spiritual and ideologies that do not acknowledge or draw on our spirituality ultimately bring out the basest dimensions of human nature. Both capitalist and communist ideologies have channelled human energy towards appeasing the appetites of the animal nature.

The economic system Bahá'ís want to create is one that is based on love for God and His creation and on interdependence between all groups of people. There are patterns of thought and behaviour in Bahá'u'lláh's system – such as the principle that work is worship, the model of combined service and supplication offered by the House of Worship, and the law of Ḥuqúqu'lláh – that make economic activity an expression of the spiritual nature of human beings. In a Bahá'í society it will be obligatory to provide all with an education that will prepare them to be 'engaged in an occupation which will profit themselves and others'.[21] Both education and work will be mandatory, with only those truly incapable of earning a living being provided subsistence. The Guardian makes reference to this interesting principle of the future World Order in the following terms:

> Every individual, no matter how handicapped and limited he may be, is under the obligation of engaging in some work or profession, for work, especially when performed in the spirit of service, is according to Bahá'u'lláh a form of worship. It has not only a utilitarian purpose, but has a value in itself, because it draws us nearer to God, and enables us to better grasp His purpose for us in this world. It is obvious, therefore, that the inheritance of wealth cannot make anyone immune from daily work.[22]

All will gain dignity and self-respect from their work and family duties, including homemaking, and none will live in dire want, although there will be differences in wealth because some diversity of condition is natural and because some will devote more energy than others to material goals. Bahá'u'lláh explains that, 'Having attained the stage of fulfilment and reached his maturity, man standeth in need of wealth'.[23] According to 'Abdu'l-Bahá, wealth is very praiseworthy when acquired legitimately by an individual's own efforts, aided by the grace of God, and if expended in ways that contribute to the well-being of humanity – such as the founding of schools, 'the encouragement of art and industry' and 'the training of orphans and the poor'.[24] Interdependence, which characterizes all of creation, is most manifest in the lives of believers, and their obedience to God's teachings would eliminate material want in the community.[25]

These teachings on the nature of work and wealth show us that many of the ways of thinking about the world which are familiar and comfortable to us – such as capitalist or social democratic or Marxist ideas about the economy, or nationalism, or adversarial political structures – are fundamentally limited by their materialistic outlook. Such systems, which today may seem natural, right and inevitable to us, are among the 'hollow and outworn institutions' and 'obsolescent doctrines and beliefs' which Shoghi Effendi said are being undermined by virtue of their own senility and inherent corruption.[26] We have grown so accustomed to materialism that it is difficult for us even to imagine that the world could be a different way. Yet Shoghi Effendi wrote that this 'cancerous materialism' affecting all parts of the world is the 'chief factor' in precipitating 'the dire ordeals and world-shaking crises' of which World War II was but 'a foretaste', and he said that this 'devouring flame' would continue to spread 'terror and consternation in the hearts of men' until humanity learns to transcend it.[27]

Dark Forces in Our Inherited Cultural Outlooks

We have to struggle to become aware of the dark forces that are part of our cultural inheritance. The way we live, the way we think and the routines of our daily lives are tainted by the forces of darkness. It is hard for us to realize how great and how serious is the effect of these forces because the world they have created is the only world we know. The Guardian said that this is the lowest ebb in all of human history, this is the darkest time, and we clearly witness that 'material forces have attacked mankind'.[28] A letter written on behalf of Shoghi Effendi expresses this thought:

> It would be perhaps impossible to find a nation or people not in a state of crisis today. The materialism, the lack of true religion and the consequent baser forces in human nature which are being released, have brought the whole world to the brink of probably the greatest crisis it has ever faced or will have to face.[29]

Part of the challenge of being a Bahá'í is to look at the attitudes, conditions and social institutions that seem ordinary to us, and understand how they are characteristic of humanity's greatest crisis.

Shoghi Effendi explicitly states that dark forces are part of the fabric of the societies in which we have grown up. They are aspects of life that we normally do not question because we have inherited them from earlier generations; they include many of the assumptions and premises by which society operates. The Guardian calls upon us to search our own hearts for signs of the presence of those pernicious forces, even in our attitude towards fellow Bahá'ís, and to subdue them through a conscious daily effort to align our personal lives more closely with the spirit of the Faith, then, secondly, to look outward and wage an ongoing battle with 'the inherited tendencies, the corruptive instincts, the fluctuating fashions' at work around us. In the passage below – penned in the context of working to eradicate negative feelings based on colour and class but which surely applies equally to negative forces of other kinds – he even points out the 'weapons' (non-political and non-violent) that will be effective in such a fight:

> Let every believer, desirous to witness the swift and healthy progress of the Cause of God, realize the twofold nature of his task. Let him first turn his eyes inwardly and search his own heart and satisfy himself that in his relations with his fellow-believers, irrespective of colour and class, he is proving himself increasingly loyal to the spirit of his beloved Faith. Assured and content that he is exerting his utmost in a conscious effort to approach nearer

every day the lofty station to which his gracious Master summons him, let him turn to his second task, and, with befitting confidence and vigour, assail the devastating power of those forces which in his own heart he has already succeeded in subduing. Fully alive to the unfailing efficacy of the power of Bahá'u'lláh, and armed with the essential weapons of wise restraint and inflexible resolve, let him wage a constant fight against the inherited tendencies, the corruptive instincts, the fluctuating fashions, the false pretences of the society in which he lives and moves.[30]

An important dimension of this statement is that the negative forces that corrode society arise from within individuals. In order to overcome the dark force of secularism we have to recognize and eliminate our own ingrained secularist attitudes. Racism, nationalism and communism are also forces of darkness; before we can rid the world of these evils, we have to rid ourselves of the racist or nationalist or materialistic tendencies that are a part of our own person. The opening stage of the battle against these forces of darkness takes place within our own heart, as we look inward to gain awareness of the ways in which some of the patterns of our own life and thinking may need correction in order for them to become fully expressive of light rather than of darkness. The next aspect of this battle is the outer one, in which we employ wisdom and constancy in striving to help others achieve a clearer vision of the principles that will ensure progress.

At this time of universal ferment and transition, all the world's cultures, along with their many positive aspects, embody elements of dark forces. Those from every background will have to evaluate their own lives and determine how their social norms differ from the standards of Bahá'u'lláh. For some, static orthodoxy and a rigid adherence to tradition are the main challenges; in other parts of the world, moral laxity and secularism are the inherited tendencies people will have to recognize in themselves. Rebellion and disorder are considered appropriate and even desirable in some modes of thought, and many cultures accept corruption as inevitable. Turning to Bahá'u'lláh's Revelation gives us the vision we need in order to become aware of the undesirable and limiting aspects of our cultures. Teaching and sharing the Cause infuses trust in God, hope in human nature and faith that this world can be transformed by spiritual forces that will overcome the darkness now clouding men's inner thoughts and enshrouding the outer world.

Bahá'u'lláh tells us to see with His eye and hear with His ear. As we read His writings our vision gradually adjusts to the light of the spirit and we become increasingly alert to negative aspects of our cultural outlook that are so subtle that initially we are not even aware of their existence.

Cultural Tendencies that Impede the Progress of the Faith

One way to understand how basic elements of our culture may express dark forces is to think about the ways that various cultural traits can slow down our personal growth and also affect the progress of the Faith. A telling example of this is the attitude, often seen in Europe and North America, and now spread widely across the globe, that religion is one specific, small dimension of life or a wholly personal phenomenon. In such a cultural environment a Bahá'í – whether he or she has found the Faith on his or her own or been born into a Bahá'í family – observes the minor role that religion plays in everyone else's life outside the Faith, and that state of affairs may seem quite natural. This believer will probably see the Bahá'í Faith as being more suited than the older religions to the needs of our times and may give it a greater role in his or her life than seems to be the case with the followers of other faiths – yet he or she may be assigning it merely the conventional position of 'religion in my life' rather than grasping its truly pivotal role at the heart of life itself. In one of the Guardian's letters a distinction is drawn between those whose religion is the Bahá'í Faith and those whose life is the Bahá'í Faith.

> There are two kinds of Bahá'ís, one might say: those whose religion is Bahá'í and those who live for the Faith. Needless to say if one can belong to the latter category, if one can be in the vanguard of heroes, martyrs and saints, it is more praiseworthy in the sight of God.[31]

The difference between those two positions must be essentially a matter of personal vision, and unless one remains very alert, personal vision can be greatly affected by the surrounding cultural milieu. It seems clear that if we are to avoid spending our brief years on earth in total aimlessness, each of us must, in effect, choose something to live for – surely the most critical choice we will ever make. Bahá'u'lláh's terse admonition on this point is: 'Seize thy chance, for it will come to thee no more.'[32]

By looking at existence through the sharp lens of the Revelation, the thinking individual will begin to perceive a coherent meaning for human life. The use of the powers of reason, in conjunction with daily reading of the sacred writings, enables us to persevere in extricating ourselves from the limitations of the prevailing world view, as 'Abdu'l-Bahá has explained:

> God has not intended man to blindly imitate his fathers and ancestors. He has endowed him with mind or the faculty of reasoning by the exercise of which he is to investigate and discover the truth; and that which he finds real and true, he must accept. He must not be an imitator or blind follower of any soul. He must not rely implicitly upon the opinion of any man without investigation; nay, each soul must seek intelligently and independently, arriving at a real conclusion and bound only by that reality. The greatest cause of bereavement and disheartening in the world of humanity is ignorance based upon blind imitation.[33]

We have seen one illustration, above, of a harmful assumption linked with thought patterns often found within a given cultural stream. In the different parts of the world there are other particular aspects of the regional cultural outlook that can impede the development of the believers and the Bahá'í community. A few other examples follow.

In some places noted for spirituality and great ethnic diversity, where religious tolerance has been actively promoted for some considerable time, it is quite easy for people to see a role for the Faith, although they can tend to think of it as yet another of those wonderful religions, all of which are good and from each of which you can choose just the bits that you especially like. In tradition-ally Catholic countries, progress can be slowed because people tend to expect someone to be the priest and be in charge. In some of the previously colonized parts of the world, people came into the Faith with the expectation that missionaries would come from the capitalist colonial centres and pay for things, so for a time they sat back and waited for that to happen. There are other areas in which a very restrictive centralized form of government has been the pattern, with most people becoming extremely hesitant to show any sign of original thinking or individual initiative and this constraining tendency can be carried over into the affairs of the Bahá'í community.

In a few cases it appears – probably through unconscious racial and ethnic prejudices inherited from the society in which they grew up – that individuals intending to serve the Faith by moving to another country have afterwards been slow to fully recognize the capacity of the local friends, which can be a tremendous obsta-cle to the development of all concerned. In some sectors, though people are fully able to read and write, there is little general tradi-tion of reading and studying outside a school setting so, rather than learning the skill of sustaining their own spiritual enthusi-asm by absorbing the teachings directly from the original books, people have tended to rely on a few studious members of the community to 'interpret' the Revelation to them and to inspire them with stories from the history of our Faith. Inherited cultural attitudes of many different kinds have slowed the progress of the Faith in different regions of the world.

Conversely, it sometimes happens that teachers who have suc-ceeded in eliminating many of the barriers of their own cultural background and personal character, becoming very pure chan-nels for the energies of the Faith, have had a notable impact on an entire national community, helping greatly to increase its spiritual vitality and awareness. Such teachers' spiritual vision has assisted the friends in their community to break through the commonly accepted regional view of what life is and what religion is. The Guardian has often highly praised such believers. The power of the Faith flows most freely when the Bahá'ís actively strive to transcend 'the inherited tendencies, the corruptive instincts, the fluctuating fashions' and 'the false pretenses' of the societies in which we live.[34]

The Source of Illumination

Belief in an innate 'goodness of human nature' can be a subtle form of irreligion. The Universal House of Justice, in *The Promise of World Peace*, states that the possibility of creating peace rests on awareness of the positive capacities of human beings but those human potentialities are not automatically realized. People have always – by struggle and free will, by exertion and endeavour – had to win their portion of goodness. The unfailing efficacy of the power of Bahá'u'lláh sustains us when we make that effort. Bahá'u'lláh describes the capacities that are latent in human nature. He says that the light of the lamp will never shine unless it is lit, and the needed power, the source of light, comes from outside the lamp. Once human beings turn to the light of God and recognize it, their character becomes illumined and they receive the energy to sustain their efforts towards goodness.

> Upon the inmost reality of each and every created thing He hath shed the light of one of His names, and made it a recipient of the glory of one of His attributes. Upon the reality of man, however, He hath focused the radiance of all of His names and attributes, and made it a mirror of His own Self. Alone of all created things man hath been singled out for so great a favour, so enduring a bounty.[35]

> These energies with which the Day Star of Divine bounty and Source of heavenly guidance hath endowed the reality of man lie, however, latent within him, even as the flame is hidden within the candle and the rays of light are potentially present in the lamp. The radiance of these energies may be obscured by worldly desires even as the light of the sun can be concealed beneath the dust and dross which cover the mirror. Neither the candle nor the lamp can be lighted through their own unaided efforts, nor can

it ever be possible for the mirror to free itself from its dross. It is clear and evident that until a fire is kindled the lamp will never be ignited, and unless the dross is blotted out from the face of the mirror it can never represent the image of the sun nor reflect its light and glory.[36]

Means of kindling the flame and polishing the mirror that is the soul will be discussed more fully in the next chapters but it is clear that the sustaining energy that human beings most need in order to create love and happiness, whether in a family, a community, a nation or the emerging world civilization, comes from love of God. Since none of us is perfect, it is inevitable that we will sometimes confront choices that may lead us to act in ways that are selfish. The person who is trying to be good, all alone without God, is surely at a great disadvantage here and is missing the strongest possible source of inner support in facing up to his or her negative inclinations.

The believer is led by sacred writings that advise him to 'Bring thyself to account each day'[37] and to 'Recite . . . the verses of God every morn and eventide'.[38] One of the great benefits of observing such exhortations is that in those daily moments of reflection one is actively encouraged to keep striving for the divine standard of conduct. By reading from the verses of God morning and evening, one is not simply refreshed by beautiful and positive thoughts but is brought into direct and frequent contact with the uniquely transformative power of the creative Word. More will be said in chapter 8 about this truly remarkable force but it is easy to see that reflecting daily on the many exhortations offered us will serve to awaken the soul gently to greater loving-kindness and social responsibility.

The believer also has recourse to prayer, in order to ask God for guidance, patience, strength – and sometimes forgiveness. Prayer and daily readings are of immense assistance in keeping up one's morale and in maintaining focus on living a harmonious and worthwhile life.

'Abdu'l-Bahá wrote that 'self-love is kneaded into the very clay of man'[39] and religion is the only force strong enough to overcome it. The world we live in is so deeply irreligious that many people have grown up unaware of the power of God in human affairs. One aspect of teaching the Faith is explaining that there is another higher level on which we can live our lives, that there is a loving God who is conscious of His creation, and that recognizing His existence creates joy, contentment and an increase of capacity within us.

In this chapter we have discussed the forces of darkness, the negative patterns of thought and behaviour that arise when human beings fail to subdue their lower nature. We have considered how our world is pervaded by irreligion, materialism and the dark forces which arise from them. We have seen that the first stage of our battle against these forces of darkness is to conquer them within ourselves. A truthful evaluation of our own thoughts and character is a wholesome, healing step to take, for it is only when we are honest about ourselves that we begin to change and can then have a profound effect on society. Prayerfully turning our attention to our own shortcomings and telling ourselves the truth need not have a negative or destructive effect; this is the beginning of a powerful, positive process when it is motivated by the love of God and the desire to be of service to humanity.

7

Combatting Forces of Darkness

The vitality of men's belief in God is dying out in every land; nothing short of His wholesome medicine can ever restore it. The corrosion of ungodliness is eating into the vitals of human society; what else but the Elixir of His potent Revelation can cleanse and revive it? *Bahá'u'lláh*[1]

An active, direct and energetic confrontation of the forces of darkness is necessary in order to create a spiritual civilization. The Bahá'í writings urge us, in unequivocal terms, to do battle against the forces of darkness. We are called upon to 'assail' them, to 'combat' them, to 'launch offensives' against them. Though in no sense a negative or violent enterprise, this offensive is strikingly new and wonderfully revolutionary.

According to Bahá'í understanding, the most effective way to assail the world's dark forces is to enlist, embody and disseminate potent spiritual energies, the chief expression of which is love. In the same way that darkness is conquered very effectively by the presence of light, so too is ignorance displaced by learning, materialism overpowered by attraction to the divine Kingdom; racism vanquished and erased through knowledge, love and respect; hatred conquered with sincere love and patience.

I charge you all that each one of you concentrate all the thoughts of your heart on love and unity. When a thought of war comes, oppose it by a stronger thought of peace. A thought of hatred must be destroyed by a more powerful thought of love.[2]

By extending the forces of light, we banish forces of darkness. In this chapter and the next, close consideration is given to the most effective ways of combatting dark forces and acquiring a greater degree of this powerful light of the spirit. The more we can draw on it, the more equipped we will be to counter forces of darkness, to engage successfully in the struggle against them and to transmit this radiance to others.

Spiritual Armaments

Heroes are they, O my Lord, lead them to the field of battle.[3]

The writings not only make it clear that we must battle against the forces of darkness, they also tell us how to obtain the 'arms' that are needed in order to assure victory. In the previous chapter mention was made of two of the weapons – wise restraint and inflexible resolve – that Shoghi Effendi refers to as essential in what should be the 'constant fight' against dark forces. It is a useful exercise to search the Bahá'í teachings for other such indications. These bellicose terms may at first appear rather incongruous in a context of exhortations to love and to create harmony. Like so many other dichotomies encountered when exploring the subtle realms of truth, this bears careful examination.

It is abundantly clear that a core purpose of religion as given by God is to eliminate contention and hostility between the members of the human race. It is equally clear that the universal struggle between the forces of light and darkness within the individual soul is another element at the heart of religious faith – that this struggle is very real and that it badly needs to be understood in order to help ensure a good outcome on both fronts, internal and societal.

Over the centuries humans have experienced all too much violent conflict, including war, and have developed a descriptive terminology for it that is familiar to us all. It would be difficult to find an adult who does not know the meaning of words such as weapon, sword, shield, army, battle and fortress. We know very well what they represent in the old context. Looking at known terms in a fresh context, as is the case with so many analogies from the writings, and bringing to bear our powers of reason in order to unravel any seeming contradictions, very often leads to deeply meaningful discoveries. The following quotations readily lend themselves to such an exercise:

> Sharp must be thy sight . . . and adamant thy soul, and brass-like thy feet, if thou wishest to be unshaken by the assaults of the selfish desires that whisper in men's breasts.[4]

> 'Verily God loveth those who, as though they were a solid wall, do battle for His Cause in serried lines!' Note that He saith 'in serried lines' – meaning crowded and pressed together, one locked to the next, each supporting his fellows. To do battle, as stated in the sacred verse, doth not, in this greatest of all dispensations, mean to go forth with sword and spear, with lance and piercing arrow – but rather weaponed with pure intent, with righteous motives, with counsels helpful and effective, with godly attributes, with deeds pleasing to the Almighty, with the qualities of heaven. It signifieth education for all mankind, guidance for all men, the spreading far and wide of the sweet savours of the spirit, the promulgation of God's proofs, the setting forth of arguments conclusive and divine, the doing of charitable deeds.

> Whensoever holy souls, drawing on the powers of heaven, shall arise with such qualities of the spirit, and march in unison, rank on rank, every one of those souls will be even as one thousand . . .[5]

In this, the day of universal brotherhood, by using some of the language men have developed over the centuries to describe violent conflict, the holy writings illustrate for us how practical, how effective – how virile, in the very best sense of the word – virtue is. It underscores the vigour with which the battle against human darkness needs to be waged.

For a long time many people have thought of religion as something with which the weak harmlessly and gainlessly occupy themselves but the kind of faith that will transform the world and eliminate war requires not only a gentle manner and kind intentions but also the acquisition of great self-discipline, inner strength and vigorous concerted action.

The writings contain a great many indications of these and other such 'armaments' needed in this all-important battle, of which a sample is given in the following passages:

> The sword of a virtuous character and upright conduct is sharper than blades of steel.[6]

> This people need no weapons of destruction, inasmuch as they have girded themselves to reconstruct the world. Their hosts are the hosts of goodly deeds, and their arms the arms of upright conduct, and their commander the fear of God.[7]

> . . . should a man, all alone, arise in the name of Bahá and put on the armour of His love, him will the Almighty cause to be victorious, though the forces of earth and heaven be arrayed against him.[8]

> The sword of wisdom is hotter than summer heat, and sharper than blades of steel, if ye do but understand. Draw it forth in My name and through the power of My might, and conquer, then, with it the cities of the hearts of them that have secluded themselves in the stronghold of their corrupt desires.[9]

> Reliance on God is indeed the strongest and safest weapon which the Bahá'í teacher can carry. For by its means no earthly power can remain unconquered, and no obstacle become insuperable.[10]

> THE HOUR IS RIPE TO . . . MOUNT THE STEED OF STEADFASTNESS, UNFURL THE BANNER OF RENUNCIATION, DON THE ARMOUR OF UTTER CONSECRATION TO GOD'S CAUSE, GIRD THEMSELVES WITH THE GIRDLE OF A CHASTE AND HOLY LIFE, UNSHEATHE THE SWORD OF BAHÁ'U'LLÁH'S UTTERANCE, BUCKLE ON THE SHIELD OF HIS LOVE, CARRY AS SOLE PROVISION IMPLICIT TRUST IN HIS PROMISE . . .[11]

Spiritual Discipline in the Individual's Battle

Means for attracting an outpouring of luminous spiritual energies are provided by Bahá'u'lláh and elucidated by 'Abdu'l-Bahá and Shoghi Effendi. There are several strategies that will enable us to be effective in the struggle against the lower forces, with the means overlapping and intertwining in subtle ways. In certain instances we stand to benefit from and assist one another, while in other instances we are required to do battle individually.

The opening stage of the individual's battle against forces of darkness involves turning one's eyes inward. This is in order to be sure that we are exerting our utmost in a conscious and continuing effort to identify and eliminate the traces of negative or godless forces within ourselves, replacing them with the positive strengths of the spirit from on high and bringing our actions increasingly into alignment with the divine standard. Bahá'u'lláh Himself advises us to:

> Set before thine eyes God's unerring Balance and, as one standing in His Presence, weigh in that Balance thine actions every day, every moment of thy life. Bring thyself to account ere thou art summoned to a reckoning...[12]

Inner discipline is an essential tool because combatting dark forces requires asserting the dominance of our higher nature over our lower. The lower aspect of our being is all too comfortable with materialism, egotism and suspicion. Spiritual discipline is the antidote to the dark forces with which we are all infected to some degree, and Shoghi Effendi told the American believers that demonstrating this transformation was their mission. Noting that Bahá'í administrative institutions developed first in North America not because of any special merit but because of the potential contrast of their efforts with the 'excessive and binding materialism' of their society, he explained:

> It is by such means as this that Bahá'u'lláh can best demonstrate to a heedless generation His almighty power to raise up from

the very midst of a people, immersed in a sea of materialism, a prey to one of the most virulent and long-standing forms of racial prejudice, and notorious for its political corruption, lawlessness and laxity in moral standards, men and women who, as time goes by, will increasingly exemplify those essential virtues of self-renunciation, of moral rectitude, of chastity, of indiscriminating fellowship, of holy discipline, and of spiritual insight that will fit them for the preponderating share they will have in calling into being that World Order and that World Civilization of which their country, no less than the entire human race, stands in desperate need.[13]

While amplified within the North American context, the message of course resonates throughout the world. In another passage, Shoghi Effendi states that:

> . . . renunciation, tenacity, dauntlessness and passionate fervour that can alone brave the dangers and sweep away the obstacles with which an infant Faith, struggling against vested interests and face to face with the entrenched forces of prejudice, of ignorance and fanaticism, must needs contend.[14]

Cultivating these spiritual strengths will enable us to overcome the dark forces that surround and infect us, and free us to participate in creating a world society. In the words of 'Abdu'l-Bahá:

> Strain every nerve to acquire both inner and outer perfections, for the fruit of the human tree hath ever been and will ever be perfections both within and without. It is not desirable that a man be left without knowledge or skills, for he is then but a barren tree. Then, so much as capacity and capability allow, ye needs must deck the tree of being with fruits such as knowledge, wisdom, spiritual perception and eloquent speech.[15]

The Guardian feels certain that no matter how much your heart may be afflicted at the sight of the difficulties now confronting the American Community, and however revolting may appear to you the attitude and the shortcomings of certain of its members, you will far from being discouraged be stimulated to exert every effort in your power to remedy such unhealthy conditions, confident that in your earnest and sincere attempt to do so, you will be assisted and guided by the unfailing confirmations of Bahá'u'lláh.[16]

Taking Responsibility for the Darkness within Ourselves

Bahá'í beliefs require people to take responsibility for the evil within themselves and in the world. The teaching that there is no external source of evil, no Satan, means that human beings are responsible for making the world the way it is and that human beings are capable of changing it.

If we are in a negative state, we have to realize that we have allowed the lower forces of nature to gain dominion over the light of God in our own character, and we have to do something about it. We cannot blame some outside power. We have to examine ourselves and perceive the dark forces that may have affected us. It is possible for a person's character to be dominated by prejudices or passion, by suspicion or hatred or, again, by self-righteousness.

These are negative conditions indicating a spiritual deficit. From time to time an individual Bahá'í will go through a very difficult period, becoming still or apathetic, and this is something that the person has to fight against – through earnest prayer and careful daily reading of the writings. Something similar can happen to a community. We have seen that the dark forces mentioned by Shoghi Effendi can become ingrained in patterns of thought and behaviour, which we might tend to incorporate into our lives when growing up in a society that has turned away from God. If, while bringing ourselves to account each day as prescribed by Bahá'u'lláh, we find some of these conditions within us, we need to make a renewed effort to connect ourselves with the sources of spiritual strength that will enable us to conquer those forces, first in our own souls, and then in the world at large.

It is often easy to attribute the world's problems to remote and powerful causes beyond human control. Some people blame the 'military-industrial complex', 'big business' or 'the multi-nationals'; in other quarters the culprit is seen as 'the liberals', 'the great powers' or 'the corrupt politicians'. Some may think the real problems stem from 'the capitalists' or 'the class system' or 'the neo-colonialists.' Only when the individuals composing human society begin to understand that the real source of negativity is within human nature and that we each have the capacity to express a more exalted reality, however, can humanity as a whole effectively come to grips with the enormous problems of the world and begin to solve them.

For this reason Shoghi Effendi characterized Bahá'í teaching campaigns as an offensive against the forces of darkness. He called on the pioneers in the Seven Year Plan to 'launch an offensive against the powers of darkness, of corruption, and of ignorance'[17] in the regions where they were to settle. Admonishing a believer who wrote about retreating from the world to ponder the writings of Bahá'u'lláh, Shoghi Effendi stated in a letter written on his behalf, 'No true and faithful Bahá'í should in this day remain idle or seek what would give him comfort or even inner satisfaction. We should be constantly assailing the forces of darkness that have enveloped the earth and hasten the dawn of the new day foretold by Bahá'u'lláh.'[18]

Whether this is something that gives us satisfaction or is the most comfortable or enjoyable prospect is irrelevant. Our responsibility is to constantly assail the forces of darkness, both within ourselves and within society, so that mankind can enter into a new phase of human development. Though we do not know for certain the exact time frame – three centuries, perhaps four – we do know a stage is approaching wherein we will no longer have the honour, the inestimable privilege of introducing a soul to the Revelation of Bahá'u'lláh for the first time. Thankfully for us at present, however, such opportunities abound. We need simply arise, undaunted, and seize them. If we assume that responsibility, ultimately we will share in the promised peace and joy of the entire family of man. If we ignore it, the opportunity will pass us by, others will do the work and we will inevitably be left with the sting of remorse.

By applying this same formula more broadly, when struggling

against a negative tendency within oneself, it can be extremely helpful to work at pinpointing its opposite quality or condition, which can serve as a spiritual 'antidote'. This must surely be one of the most fitting and fruitful uses of one's intellect – 'the rational faculty',[19] 'this divinely ordained and subtle Reality, this sign of the revelation of the All-Abiding, All-Glorious God'.[20] By reflecting deeply on the specific problem with the focus of, 'What virtue, if I had it in greater degree, would help to extinguish this particular shortcoming?' a specific spiritual remedy can be identified, or often more than one. Having settled on an antidote, one can then be alert to every mention of that virtue in the writings, looking for clues about ways in which to cultivate it in one's own daily life.

While it's essential to strive our utmost to transform our character, it is also wise to expect setbacks to occur and not to paralyse our own efforts by being too self-critical. Surely the important thing – after doing, saying or thinking something we wish we had not – is to pick ourselves up again, pray for forgiveness and greater strength, and persevere in our effort to improve. Tests reveal the smudges on the mirror of our heart and also reveal our relative powerlessness. That can be discouraging but unless we had an overly inflated idea of our own inner strength and perfection to start with, tests should serve as a healthy reality check.

> These tests, even as thou didst write, do but cleanse the spotting of self from off the mirror of the heart, till the Sun of Truth can cast its rays thereon; for there is no veil more obstructive than the self, and however tenuous that veil may be, at the last it will completely shut a person out, and deprive him of his portion of eternal grace.[21]

Personal spiritual discipline is a necessary element in winning victory over the lower self – discipline in the sense of harnessing the will and focusing attention in order to harmonize, adjust and control one's natural inclinations. The writings are full of exhortations to 'exert' ourselves and that may be as good a definition of spiritual discipline as any. To exert oneself, according to common definitions, is to take action, to make sustained and untiring effort, to try hard.

It is also essential that we keep our thoughts and feelings focused on the wonderful, positive potential of individual souls and of the world. The spiritual energies released by Bahá'u'lláh for the creation of a new society cannot operate through us if we are overcome by negative forces.

The harder we strive to attain our goal, 'the greater will be the confirmations of Bahá'u'lláh', and the 'more certain' we can feel of obtaining success. We should thus be cheerful, and exert ourselves with 'full faith and confidence'. Bahá'u'lláh has 'promised His Divine assistance to every one who arises with a pure and detached heart to spread His Holy Word' – 'even though he may be bereft of every human knowledge and capacity' – 'notwithstanding the forces of darkness and of opposition which may be arrayed against him'. 'The goal is clear, the path safe and certain, and the assurances of Bahá'u'lláh as to the eventual success of our efforts quite emphatic.' Through firmness, and whole-hearted effort we can 'carry on the great work which He has entrusted into our hands'.[22]

We have seen that the dark forces mentioned by Shoghi Effendi can become ingrained in patterns of thought and behaviour that we incorporate into our lives when growing up in a society that has turned away from God. If, while bringing ourselves to account each day as prescribed by Bahá'u'lláh, we find some of these conditions within us, we need to connect ourselves with the sources of spiritual strength that will enable us to conquer those forces. While this is not to say that we need to wait to become perfect before trying to help in the transformation of society, we should not lose sight of the fact that the area in which we can effect immediate changes, the field where we have the greatest scope for action, is in improving our own attitudes and conduct. If we do not take action to make changes within ourselves, no one else will do it for us.

Seeking Divine Assistance to Combat Dark Forces

We fight the dark forces in ourselves by opening the channels through which God's love and power can flow through us.

There are dark forces in the world today of despair and hatred and suspicion; the believers must, as the Master said, turn their backs on these and their faces to Him, confident of His help and protection.[23]

A sincere intention to serve and obey Bahá'u'lláh draws us out of the negative condition in which we may find ourselves. He stands ready to help us in this endeavour. 'Abdu'l-Bahá is reported to have explained that just as the earth attracts everything downward by the force of gravity, so also the pull of man's lower self will, without divine assistance, necessarily override efforts to soar. No matter how many times and with how much effort we throw an object upward, it will soon come down. The only way for something to stay up is for it to come under the influence of energies acting with greater strength than that of earth's gravity. The bird stays aloft as long as its life force can make use of muscular strength to move its wings and it can take advantage of air currents. If the bird loses its connection with those superior sources of power, the force of gravity immediately pulls it down. Spiritual power is the only force capable of freeing human beings from the captivity of the world.

Just as the earth attracts everything to the centre of gravity, and every object thrown upward into space will come down, so also material ideas and worldly thoughts attract man to the centre of self. Anger, passion, ignorance, prejudice, greed, envy, covetousness, jealousy and suspicion prevent man from ascending to the realms of holiness, imprisoning him in the claws of self and the cage of egotism. The physical man, unassisted by the divine power, trying to escape from one of these invisible enemies, will unconsciously fall into the hands of another. No sooner does he attempt to soar upward than the density of the love of self, like the power of gravity, draws him to the earth. The only power that is capable of delivering man from this captivity is the power of the breaths of the Holy Spirit. The attraction of the power of the Holy Spirit is so effective that it keeps man ever on the path of upward ascension. The malevolent forces of no enemy will touch those sanctified souls who have made this universal power their guide. With tranquil heart and assured spirit they are flying upward day and night, journeying through the illimitable space of the teachings of Bahá'u'lláh.[24]

Relying upon the power of the Faith releases people from the entrapment of selfish and negative forces.

Another image that helps us to understand this spiritual principle depicts the condition of iron in the forge, being subjected to the influence of flame. When the iron of the soul is under the transforming influence of spiritual fire, it takes on the very characteristics of fire. It begins to glow with the warmth of the power of Bahá'u'lláh. Then, instead of being dark and cold and solid, it becomes luminous, full of heat, malleable or even fluid in character. It is still iron, but it is in a completely different condition. If the iron is taken away from the heat it begins to assume its old character again. It is a constant struggle. We cannot say, 'Now I have got it all heated up and melted, I can relax a bit', because soon the spiritual iron of the soul will cool down and resume its old condition. There has to be someone busy with the forge, seeing to it that the divine fire is blazing all the time. We defeat the forces of darkness when we provide the conditions for our heart to be ignited with the fire of the love of God and when we feed that flame with prayer, meditation, study of the holy Word and continuous service to others.

The next step is to turn our being towards God and earnestly seek divine assistance in our effort to progress. These two measures prepare us to become increasingly effective when turning our attention outward to help heal the society in which we live. This three-step process – inward examination, asking God's assistance and finally outward action – though it needs to be repeated ceaselessly, is ever fresh and absorbing. It takes new form and meaning as the circumstances of our lives constantly present new challenges. One of the blessings of interaction with others is that it effectively reveals to us our shortcomings and thus enables us to work on them. In the course of this journey to subdue self, we will be able to take joy in the little signs that progress is being made, and that will encourage us to continue.

Just as the Cause of God as a whole passes through periods of crisis which, after considerable effort, are followed by victory, so also our individual lives seem to follow a similar pattern. It helps to recognize this, to realize that crises and periods of difficulty are to be expected in the course of one's earthly existence, and that – if faced in the right way – each test or trial will lead us to greater understanding and spiritual maturity.

In this chapter we have examined the ways we can fight the forces of darkness. We begin by acknowledging that people's actions are causing the world's problems and that people's actions, including our own, can solve them. The next step is to make efforts to eliminate the negative tendencies within ourselves. Turning to God gives us access to the power we need to overcome the forces of darkness, and spiritual discipline gives us sustained strength and perseverance for this endeavour. When we replace negative thoughts, feelings and actions with profitable and constructive ones, the power of Bahá'u'lláh can be reflected in us, flow through us and influence the world.

The following chapter details a number of ways we can each, individually and collectively as members of neighbourhoods and communities, act, not only to battle the forces of darkness surrounding us but to kindle and champion the forces of light which are omnipresent and stand ever-ready for willing and committed custodians.

8

Custodians of the Forces of Light

> In short, whatsoever thing is arranged in harmony and with love
> and purity of motive, its result is light, and should the least trace of
> estrangement prevail the result shall be darkness upon darkness.
> *'Abdu'l-Bahá*[1]

The powers and energies streaming from the Manifestation of
God transform those souls that turn towards Him. These powers
animate, vivify and ennoble us and create within us the capacity,
in turn, to quicken the society in which we live. In this chapter
we consider what actions can be taken to draw more fully on the
divine forces that have come into the world through Bahá'u'lláh
and how we can enhance our ability to transmit those forces to
others.

It is a tremendous privilege for us to know that such a source of
confirmation and divine assistance is at hand. This puts us in quite
a different position from the other people in the world because
we can consciously connect ourselves to these forces and let them
work through us. Pilgrims reported that Shoghi Effendi had told
them that Bahá'ís were not drawing enough on the power of the
Cause, so a great reservoir of confirmations had accumulated,
with torrents of celestial energies built up and waiting under pressure, meaning that whatever anyone did for the Cause attracted a
tremendous outpouring of divine bounty. In one of his messages
he said that the doubter should arise and test the existence of the
powers available to assist their efforts:

God's own Plan has been set in motion. It is gathering momentum with every passing day. The powers of heaven and earth mysteriously assist in its execution. Such an opportunity is irreplaceable. Let the doubter arise and himself verify the truth of such assertions. To try, to persevere, is to insure ultimate and complete victory.[2]

And in another message he affirms that:

So powerful will be the effusions of Divine grace . . . that its members will find themselves overpowered by the evidences of their regenerative power.[3]

Making use of these regenerative energies in our lives involves us in a series of related processes that lead into and intensify each other. Our love of Bahá'u'lláh increases our eagerness to live the Bahá'í life and creates in us a thirst for spirituality. The divine Word satisfies that thirst and at the same time enables us to transform our character and our behaviour. It reorients the direction of our lives. It channels our actions so that they harmonize with the processes God has set in motion in the world. The impulse we receive from the divine creative energies of the Word of God moves through us and on to others. When our lives express the divine purpose for which we have been created, we experience joy and our ability to love God and humanity expands. We become more and more consecrated to the will of God as expressed in Bahá'u'lláh's Revelation and so our quest for spirituality increases, while the quality of our actions is enhanced.

Our Interactions with Others

In one of the most important and useful quotations that was encountered in this study, Shoghi Effendi, writing through a secretary, warns the Bahá'ís that we should be on our guard lest we allow dark forces to enter into our lives by feeling or thinking negatively about each other. This is an amazing statement. He does not ask us just to watch what we say and how we act but expects us to reach deeper, going beyond those obvious tasks, and not allow ourselves to harbour negative thoughts or resentment towards our fellows.

> The world is full of evil and dark forces and the friends must not permit these forces to get hold of them by thinking and feeling negatively towards each other . . .[4]

There is a very helpful – and very challenging – passage from one of 'Abdu'l-Bahá's talks that touches on this vital subject:

> You must manifest complete love and affection toward all man-kind. Do not exalt yourselves above others, but consider all as your equals, recognizing them as the servants of one God. Know that God is compassionate toward all; therefore, love all from the depths of your hearts, prefer all religionists before yourselves, be filled with love for every race, and be kind toward the people of all nationalities. Never speak disparagingly of others, but praise without distinction. Pollute not your tongues by speaking evil of another. Recognize your enemies as friends, and consider those who wish you evil as the wishers of good. You must not see evil as evil and then compromise with your opinion, for to treat in a smooth, kindly way one whom you consider evil or an enemy is hypocrisy, and this is not worthy or allowable. You must consider your enemies as your friends, look upon your evil-wishers as your well-wishers and treat them accordingly. Act in such a way that your heart may be free from hatred. Let not your heart be offended with anyone. If some one commits an error and wrong toward you, you must instantly forgive him. Do not complain of others. Refrain from reprimanding them, and if you wish to give admonition or advice, let it be offered in such a way that it will not burden the bearer. Turn all your thoughts toward bringing joy to hearts. Beware! Beware! lest ye offend any heart. Assist the world of humanity as much as possible. Be the source of consolation to every sad one, assist every weak one, be helpful to every indigent one, care for every sick one, be the cause of glorification to every lowly one, and shelter those who are overshadowed by fear.
>
> In brief, let each one of you be as a lamp shining forth with

the light of the virtues of the world of humanity. Be trustworthy, sincere, affectionate and replete with chastity. Be illumined, be spiritual, be divine, be glorious, be quickened of God, be a Bahá'í.[5]

The vitalizing energies of Bahá'u'lláh's Revelation can shape us into an expression of His intention for humanity, if only we orient ourselves towards Him and attempt to conform to His teachings. They can have little effect on us if we allow ourselves to remain frozen in the negative patterns of interaction that characterize a decadent society. The Guardian warned that 'when Bahá'ís permit the dark forces of the world to enter into their own relationships within the Faith they gravely jeopardize its progress'.[6] Love and unity in the Bahá'í community are expressions of the will of God. When we reinforce these qualities, we become channels of spiritual power. If we diminish those qualities in any way – even through negative thoughts and feelings – we impair our connection with the spiritual forces animating the world.

It is helpful to perceive each other as a manifestation of divine purpose. Each human reality is an emanation from God, a unique reflection of the names of God. Let us regard each other as a sign of the reality of God, full of truths and mysteries through which we can unravel the secrets of creation.

Negative thoughts and feelings lower our sights to the plane of all the limitations of this nether world. Positive thoughts and loving feelings expand our capacity and understanding to a higher level.

The spiritual principle that negative thoughts and feelings block the possibility of transformation applies to society as a whole, as well as to interpersonal relations. This principle allows us to understand why protest movements are a less effective strategy for social change than attempting to provide a model for social evolution, which is the Bahá'í approach. Protesting against racism or environmental degradation or economic injustice usually focuses attention on the present and its imperfections instead of on the future and its potentialities. It does not create a positive dynamic for social change. Often protest movements, however well-intentioned, fall into negative patterns that create bitterness, estrangement and sometimes even violence, among the elements of society where change is needed.

Bahá'ís are occasionally accused of naive idealism or utopian impracticality because of our unwillingness to engage in partisan politics and protests. One way to respond to these accusations is to explain that we believe that the most useful response to social problems is to demonstrate that other ways of doing things are possible and workable. The Bahá'í approach to social problems is not naive: we are actively trying to understand the forces of darkness and to implement new models capable of truly safeguarding the fundamental, spiritual and long-term needs of humanity. It is neither escapist nor impractical: our standard is to find and eliminate these forces within ourselves – a highly challenging and lifelong task – and to create new and vital social forms that transcend the negative tendencies of our inherited cultures. In so doing we provide society with a peerless and essential map.

The response to the dark force of racism is an example of the power of the Bahá'í approach. It is possible to feel anger about social and racial injustice – even to take an action such as participating in a protest march – without discovering one's own racial or ethnic prejudices or changing the segregated patterns of one's own life. The Bahá'í strategies for fighting the forces of darkness require more from the individual. Every believer of every race has to look within his or her own heart and mind to find the subconscious and unquestioned racist attitudes that we have inevitably absorbed to some degree. Relying on the power of faith, we have to root out those attitudes and establish patterns of friendship, work relationships and social activities that go against the society's norms of racial bias and segregation. Bahá'í communities that have made noteworthy progress on this path have sometimes been seen to generate tremendous interest and enthusiasm in the society around them. Shoghi Effendi, writing through his secretary to a Bahá'í community in the southern United States in 1947, described the nature of the battle against the forces of darkness:

> The friends must, at all times, bear in mind that they are, in a way, like soldiers under attack. The world is at present in an

exceedingly dark condition spiritually; hatred and prejudice, of every sort, are literally tearing it to pieces. We, on the other hand, are the custodians of the opposite forces, the forces of love, of unity, of peace and integration, and we must constantly be on our guard, whether as individuals or as an Assembly or Community, lest through us these destructive, negative forces enter into our midst. In other words we must beware lest the darkness of society become reflected in our acts and attitudes, perhaps all unconsciously. Love for each other, the deep sense that we are a new organism, the dawn-breakers of a New World Order, must constantly animate our Bahá'í lives, and we must pray to be protected from the contamination of a society which is so diseased with prejudice.[7]

When Shoghi Effendi told the Bahá'ís that we must not permit dark forces to take hold of us by thinking and feeling negatively towards each other, he set a standard for our interaction with each other and with the world.

Transmitting Divine Power to Others

As we draw on the energies of the Revelation to transform ourselves and to bring sense to a chaotic world, it is essential that we share our knowledge of those forces with others. Shoghi Effendi tells us that our awareness of the power of Bahá'u'lláh acting in the world gives us an inescapable responsibility:

The impetus that has been given by the Manifestation of God for this Age is the sole one that can regenerate humanity, and as we Bahá'ís are the only ones yet aware of this new force in the world, our obligation towards our fellow men is tremendous and inescapable![8]

What would it be like not to know anything about the coming of the Manifestation of God, the bursting of His spirit upon the world, the action of the forces released by Him in the breakdown of an outmoded society and the building up of a new World Order?

How could we, a relative handful of people on the face of the planet who do have a basic understanding of it, be complacent and leave the rest of humanity floundering in the darkness, in agony? Our responsibility towards our fellow men is immense. Likewise, the responsibility of people, once they have learned of the Faith, is grave. If they have not heard of it, the Bahá'ís are answerable for not having offered it to them. The judgement works both ways.

When we teach the Faith, we should do so in a way that demonstrates the transforming power of the energies we have been examining here. Shoghi Effendi calls the Bahá'í teacher to 'demonstrate the creative and transforming potency of the Faith we profess'.[9] We should not think that we are fulfilling the requirement of Bahá'u'lláh to teach His Faith simply by offering information, by giving out pamphlets and flatly explaining that the Bahá'í Faith is about this and about that, as in, 'I only present you with some facts and you can do what you want about it.' That is too uncommitted a way of presenting the Faith. It has been made incumbent upon the believers to 'diffuse the divine fragrances',[10] to 'breathe life into others',[11] to 'bestow spirit upon mouldering bones, give sight to the blind, balm and freshness to the depressed, and liveliness and grace to the dispirited'.[12] This is what we are called on to do. When we face a soul in the teaching work, we have to think how we can awaken the seed of the spirit, latent in the soul of this individual. We know that only the fire of the love of God is going to be able to do that and it will probably depend on us to a great degree. The love that we have for God will allow us to focus on that seed and to stimulate its growth. If we ourselves are not transformed through the potency of this creative force, how shall we be able to accomplish that delicate feat? How can the poor give to the poor?

'Abdu'l-Bahá tells us that to the degree a soul loves God, to that degree will he move and affect the heart of his listener.[13] The Word has a power in itself. He gives the example of Judas Iscariot teaching and bringing people to the recognition of Christ, stating that this was due to the power of the Word, not to that of Judas. However, if this power inherent in the Word is combined with living the life, then it has a most penetrating influence. And instead of thinking, 'What is the matter with people? Why are they not receptive? I tell so many people about the Faith but nobody pays attention,' we should think of each person as a precious gift that has come to us from God and consider how we can manage to spark the heart to life. When we are with those souls, we inwardly pray for them. After we speak with them, even though they may have initially rejected the message, we are not to leave them entirely to themselves but continue to ask divine blessings for them. Perhaps those spiritually enlightened thoughts shared, the loving-kindness expressed, will begin to act upon them in some quiet moment when they are alone and the conversation will come back to them. Perhaps that seed fell on fertile soil and our prayers will attract the rain of blessings to gradually awaken it to life.

Bahá'u'lláh calls upon each believer to 'Be ablaze as the fire, that ye may burn away the veils of heedlessness and set aglow, through the quickening energies of the love of God, the chilled and wayward heart'.[14] He guides us to be enkindled when we are teaching the Faith, call on His name, cast aside our shortcomings, place our whole trust in Him and, ablaze with the fire of His love, touch the hearts of our listeners. In the writings we have been given instructions for kindling this flame within our own soul, as well as prayers for assistance and confirmation in this task.

> O Friends! You must all be so ablaze in this day with the fire of the love of God that the heat thereof may be manifest in all your veins, your limbs and members of your body, and the peoples of the world may be ignited by this heat and turn to the horizon of the Beloved.[15]

It may at times be difficult to recognize who, of the many individuals whose paths we cross in our daily lives, might be receptive to Bahá'u'lláh's message and whether or not those we have taught have been influenced in hearing this message. We are told by Bahá'u'lláh that misbelief, faith and iniquity can all be perceived from a person's face[16] and the Master reiterates the thought:

> When the heart hath become clear and pure then the face will become illuminated, because the face is the mirror of the heart.[17]

This would seem to imply that the condition evident in a person's face alone should show whether that individual has accepted the Manifestation of God and whether or not he or she is striving to live in accord with the divine teachings. When the soul is on fire, ablaze and luminous with the light of the love of God, then something is communicated through the expression of the eyes, is reflected in that external mirror of the inner state – and will attract receptive hearts. This is the light we see in one another when we are in a condition of spiritual receptivity. The joy of the light one feels from God, compounded by the illumination reflected from the inner being of spiritually like-minded friends, reverberates back and forth between the mirrors of the hearts. This is bliss. This is heaven. This is true unity, the Abhá paradise we want to spread from pole to pole across the planet.

In the Tablets of the Divine Plan, 'Abdu'l-Bahá calls upon the believers to become incarnate light.[18] This is an amazing requirement for teaching. The light that we want to spread to others has to shine in our own being. We should assume an attitude of spiritual radiance, we should pray for it, we should trust that that light is going to shine in us when we open our lips and speak of the Faith. This will have a great influence in our teaching work. Those who are effective teachers sometimes recount experiencing this great power moving within them. How can seekers be moved if we ourselves are not? We ourselves should be moved by the beauty and greatness of the Faith at the time we are speaking of it. 'Abdu'l-Bahá is reported to have said, 'If one tree in a forest is aflame, how can the other trees resist?' Our mandate is to become incarnate light, to be aflame with the love of this Faith in such a way that no one can resist being attracted to that light.

As teachers we also have much to learn from those we teach. For a soul to have recognized the Manifestation of God for this Day is a supremely transformative occasion and oftentimes the teacher's own reflection of His light may have begun to dim or to be taken even slightly for granted. Being in the presence of someone so earnestly seeking and so alive and enkindled often serves to fan our own fire and spiritual thirst.

The goal of our teaching should be for the spirit of the Faith to permeate and transform the lives of those we teach. To accomplish this, a teaching effort 'unexampled in its scope and sustained vitality is urgently required so that the moving spirit of its Founder may permeate and transform the lives of the countless multitudes that hunger for its teachings'.[19] First of all, that spirit has to be moving in us. Then that moving spirit will have an effect in the hearts of those we teach and begin to permeate and transform them. Following on from this, they learn to turn to the writings directly on their own. They are weaned from the nursing that we have given them at the beginning. When an individual who recognizes the truth of the Cause becomes an 'avowed believer', the next step is to become an 'active supporter' of the Faith. Both these things are vital. The number of avowed believers needs to increase and the process through which they become 'active supporters' of the work of the Faith has to be accelerated. The current institute process is designed to meet this need.

The Universal House of Justice is calling us to effective teaching – not just teaching but teaching that results in active supporters. The process should carry through these two stages and the House of Justice has pointed out that in the course of teaching 'a declaration of Faith is merely a milestone along the way – albeit a very important one'.[20] In recent years the Bahá'í community has learned that identifying a community of interest, inviting people to participate in children's classes, junior youth programmes, study circles and devotional gatherings, and intensifying those activities through teaching campaigns, is a very effective way to ensure that support and consecration follows enrolment.

'Abdu'l-Bahá describes teaching as the greatest gift of God. Teaching attracts divine confirmations to us, confirmations that transform both our inner and outer lives and make us into new beings suited for God's Kingdom. 'God hath prescribed unto every one the duty of teaching His Cause'[21] and we cannot leave the souls we have brought to the Faith deprived of that bounty, just as we cannot deprive ourselves of it. How can we think that if we stop teaching we will continue to receive divine confirmations? The friends should be very careful that they balance any administrative activities with the teaching work. It is mainly the teaching work that energizes. Sometimes we become so busy meeting the administrative needs of the Faith that we deprive ourselves of the gifts inherent in this responsibility to give the message. It is possible to reorient the focus of our lives, even if we cannot radically change our activities. We then continue to do all the things that we are obliged to do in a day but our focus becomes finding seeking souls. We should pray in the morning to find seeking and receptive souls, ask Bahá'u'lláh to help us remain alert to opportunities during the day, beg Him to enable us to find ways that we can meet and get to know people who are longing for the Faith. This attitude gives all our other responsibilities new meaning.

We are carriers of the light of God; it must burn in our heart, shine through our being. When other people become attracted to that light, we have to devote our attention to those souls until it shines through them as well.

The Individual: Fulcrum of the World's Transformation

As we have seen in the course of this study, individual transformation and action are the means through which the plan of God comes to fruition in the world. Our activities, our exertions to draw on that power, our conscious efforts to channel it and translate it into actions, crystallize those forces released by Bahá'u'lláh into patterns and social structures that embody His will. The grace of God expresses itself in human affairs through the efforts of individual souls to know Him, love Him and serve Him.

The path of action through which we fulfil God's intention for humanity is also the path that allows us to attain our own highest stage of the excellence latent in each one of us. 'Abdu'l-Bahá explains that, while we can potentially express and reflect the light of all the names and attributes of God, there is a dominant name of God acting in every individual.[22] This is why each of us views the writings and views life from a somewhat different perspective. Perhaps the name of God the Merciful dominates in one and in another the name of God the Knower. In one person there is a tremendous thirst for knowledge while another person shows a thirst for ministering to people's needs. The unique endowment of divine spirit, which is the character of each human being, will come to light and be fully expressed through our individual efforts to serve the divine plan. Each of us has a distinct role to play, each has a unique contribution to make to the construction of a new World Order. In the final analysis, no one can play the role of anyone else or deprive another of their service.

For our own well-being, and for the sake of humanity, we need to dedicate ourselves to channelling the creative energies released by Bahá'u'lláh. In a quotation which summarizes the theme of our study, the Guardian appealed to the Bahá'ís to focus on this process:

> I entreat you, dear friends, to continue, nay, to redouble your efforts, to keep your vision clear, your hopes undimmed, your determination unshaken, so that the power of God within us may fill the world with all its glory.[23]

Divine power is on tap and available to us all. We are surrounded and permeated by celestial energies, immersed in Bahá'u'lláh's ocean of light. The writings affirm that there is no limit to His might and glory, saying that we should 'lift up the veil'[24] and strive for 'constant awareness of His Presence'.[25] Bahá'u'lláh makes it clear that God's love is the cause of our creation and that the very definition of paradise for human beings is His love.[26] For our own sake, He wants us to draw nearer to Him. The greatest possible joy and contentment will be reached through moving ever closer to the source of all bounty, beauty, peace and illumination. The only obstacle, Bahá'u'lláh tells us, is the world and He explains that 'by "the world" is meant your unawareness of Him Who is your Maker, and your absorption in aught else but Him'.[27]

When dealing with the world we need to stay alert and keep our vision clear. One of the possible pitfalls in daily life can be to muddle Bahá'u'lláh's recommendation for us to exercise moderation with His admonition not to be fanatical. In today's society, if we conform to the standard to which He calls us, some will categorize us as religious fanatics because there is such a great contrast between the divine standard and the standards of the society around us. But God's law and teachings are themselves the very essence of moderation and we cannot consider our own behaviour to be fanatical unless we exceed what Bahá'u'lláh asks of us. If we were to go beyond that and unwisely overstep the mark in ways that He has not indicated, then perhaps we could be considered to be fanatics. But we have to judge our actions in the context of God's Word:

> . . . the sublime achievements of man reside in those quali-
> ties and attributes that exclusively pertain to the angels of the
> Supreme Concourse. Therefore, when praiseworthy qualities and
> high morals emanate from man, he becometh a heavenly being,
> an angel of the Kingdom, a divine reality and a celestial efful-
> gence.[28]

If we became celestial angels, would that be fanatical?

Moderation cannot be halfway between the norms of the world and the standard of the Revelation. That definitely misses the mark. We should not delude ourselves on this point. Shoghi Effendi referred to humanity in its current stage of development as a 'generation of the half-light'.[29] Far from an excuse to remove ourselves of responsibility for the world around us, it is a lamentable fact that we must arise to remedy. Clearly, all of us are bound to fall short of the teachings repeatedly, however hard we try, but we should aim at the high mark to which Bahá'u'lláh calls us – to please God with our actions, to become truly worthy of the name human, to serve mankind the very best we can – and He has defined for us how to do that. We need to recognize that the standard of the teachings is moderation itself. It is the golden mean and the very definition of justice.

Having been given the grace of recognizing Bahá'u'lláh, should we not, according to our capacity, pour out our life, our resources and our time and pare away from our lives the trivialities, the superficial excesses and the things that one acquires by the nature of the society we inhabit? There are too few of us, the work is too great. The honour in such a life-giving renunciation is inestimable.

If we could see ourselves the way the souls on the other side see us, we would know, as we have been told, that they watch our spiritual condition and when they see us attracted and moving by the influence of this divine light they rejoice, they pray for us, they pour confirmations upon us. When they see us enshrouded in mists because of our attachments and passions they also pray for us, to deliver us from that condition.

In our investigation of the forces of our time, we have seen that the creative energies of the Word of God work in us and through us. Bahá'u'lláh has revealed the words and the power that will create a just and peaceful world civilization. We live and move and have our being through His Word. The creative, transforming energies of God gain a concrete shape in the material world through the actions we take and the institutions that we form in accordance with His will. New patterns of social action, new ways of thinking about reality and new ways of organizing human life crystallize out of His divine power through the systematic activity of those divinely ordained institutions. The vision that we are given of the remedial Hand of God working in the world enables us to understand the chaos and turbulence of a planet in transition. The lens of the Revelation gives us clarity in perceiving the forces of darkness that are also operating in society, and its standards enable us to combat them. The more we become pure reflections of the light of Bahá'u'lláh, the more successful we become in transmitting it to others.

To have recognized Bahá'u'lláh and chosen to follow Him is a station accompanied by eternal sovereignty and imperishable honour. This is what we gain from entering the Faith; the blessings that come from serving Him are even greater. 'The service of the friends', 'Abdu'l-Bahá says in a Tablet, 'belongs to God, not to them.'[30] However unworthy, we are the instruments with which He is working and are able to behold the wonder of the re-creation of the world, taking place, in part, through our services. The Revelation has brought the waters of life and if we are willing instruments, it pours through us, streaming out to our fellow human beings. Then will we stand as witnesses before the glory and greatness of God.

That is our privilege and our inheritance. It is our destiny, if we but arise to embrace it.

PART TWO

Extracts from the Writings and Messages of Shoghi Effendi on the Forces of Our Time

. . . and seek from that Source of Celestial Potency all the guidance, the spirit, the power which we shall need for the fulfilment of our mission in this life.[1]

It is our primary task to keep the most vigilant eye on the manner and character of its growth, to combat effectively the forces of separation and sectarian tendencies, lest the Spirit of the Cause be obscured, its unity be threatened, its Teachings suffer corruption; lest extreme orthodoxy on the one hand, and irresponsible freedom on the other, cause it to deviate from that Straight Path which alone can lead it to success.[2]

. . . we should form one united front and combat, wisely and tactfully, every force that might darken the spirit of the Movement, cause division in its ranks, and narrow it by dogmatic and sectarian belief.[3]

. . . you will inaugurate a brilliant and vigorous campaign of Teaching, that shall by its very splendour banish the darkness of difference and contention that so impede the majestic and onward march of the Cause in every land.[4]

. . . the ever-increasing confusion of the world, threatened as never before with disruptive forces . . .[5]

Let us pray to God that in these days of world encircling-gloom, when the dark forces of nature, of hate, rebellion, anarchy and reaction are threatening the very stability of human society, when the most precious fruits of civilization are undergoing severe and unparalleled tests, we may all realize, more profoundly than ever, that though a mere handful amidst the seething masses of the world, we are in this day the chosen instruments of God's grace, that our mission is most urgent and vital to the fate of humanity, and, fortified by these sentiments, arise to achieve God's holy purpose for mankind.[6]

Strive therefore with heart and soul to drink deep from the spirit of self-sacrifice which the pioneers of the Cause have so gloriously displayed, and equip yourselves fully to fight the good fight against the dark forces that have encompassed the world today.[7]

The plight of mankind, the condition and circumstances under which we live and labour are truly disheartening, and the darkness of prejudice and ill-will enough to chill the stoutest heart. Disillusion and dismay are invading the hearts of peoples and nations, and the hope and vision of a united and regenerated humanity is growing dimmer and dimmer every day. Time-honoured institutions, cherished ideals, and sacred traditions are suffering in these days of bewildering change, from the effects of the gravest onslaught, and the precious fruit of centuries of patient and earnest labour is faced with peril. Passions, supposed to have been curbed and subdued, are now burning fiercer than ever before, and the voice of peace and good-will seems drowned amid unceasing convulsions and turmoil. What, let us ask ourselves, should be our attitude as we stand under the all-seeing eye of our vigilant Master, gazing at a sad spectacle so utterly remote from the spirit which He breathed into the world? Are we to follow in the wake of the wayward and the despairing? Are we to allow our vision of so unique, so enduring, so precious a Cause to be clouded by the stain and dust of worldly happenings, which, no matter how glittering and far-reaching in their immediate effects, are but the fleeting shadows of an imperfect world? Are we to be carried away by the flood of hollow and conflicting ideas, or are we to stand, unsubdued and unblemished, upon the everlasting rock of God's Divine Instructions? Shall we not equip ourselves with a clear and full understanding of their purpose and implications for the age we live in, and with an unconquerable resolve arise to utilize them, intelligently and with scrupulous fidelity, for the enlightenment and the promotion of the good of all mankind?[8]

We have but to turn our eyes to the world without to realize the fierceness and the magnitude of the forces of darkness that are struggling with the dawning light of the Abhá Revelation. Nations, though exhausted and disillusioned, have seemingly begun to cherish anew the spirit of revenge, of domination, and strife. Peoples, convulsed by economic upheavals, are slowly drifting into two great opposing camps with all their menace of social chaos, class hatreds, and worldwide ruin. Races, alienated more than ever before, are filled with mistrust, humiliation and fear, and seem to prepare themselves for a fresh and fateful encounter. Creeds and religions, caught in a whirlpool of conflict and passion, appear to gaze with impotence and despair at this spectacle of unceasing turmoil.[9]

I entreat you, dear friends, to continue, nay, to redouble your efforts to keep your vision clear, your hopes undimmed, your determination unshaken, so that the power of God within us may fill the world with all its glory.[10]

We need never be disappointed with the smallness of our numbers or be discouraged at the reluctance of the majority of the people to accept the Teachings, but rather we must endeavour all the more, confident that Truth shall ultimately prevail, and that the dark forces of the world shall in time be vanquished.[11]

... such measures as will effectually conduce to a fuller recognition of the dynamic force latent in the Bahá'í Faith ...[12]

... the sublimity, the innocence, and the dynamic force of the Faith of Bahá'u'lláh ...[13]

The administrative machinery of the Cause ... should both provide the impulse whereby the dynamic forces latent in the Faith can unfold, crystallize, and shape the lives and conduct of men, and serve as a medium for the interchange of thought ...[14]

Let such remarkable revelations of the reality and continuity of the divine purpose, made manifest from time to time to us His feeble children, serve to fortify our faith in Him, to warm the chill which fleeting misfortunes may leave behind, and fill us with that celestial potency which alone can enable us to withstand the storm and stress that lives dedicated to His service must needs encounter.[15]

It will gladden and rejoice every one of you to learn that from various quarters there has of late reached the Holy Land tidings of fresh developments that are a clear indication of those hidden and transforming influences which, from the source of Bahá'u'lláh's mystic strength, continue to flow with ever-increasing vitality into the heart of this troubled world.[16]

And as I contemplate the far-reaching possibilities involved in a careful handling of those forces which Bahá'u'lláh's almighty arm has now released, I cannot help reflecting upon the dominant share which the American friends, at home as well as in distant lands, have contributed to this rejuvenation of the Cause of God, and the decisive part it is theirs to play in its eventual victory.[17]

Assured and content that he is exerting his utmost in a conscious effort to approach nearer every day the lofty station to which his gracious Master summons him, let him turn to his second task, and, with befitting confidence and vigour, assail the devastating power of those forces which in his own heart he has already succeeded in subduing. Fully alive to the unfailing efficacy of the power of Bahá'u'lláh, and armed with the essential weapons of wise restraint and inflexible resolve, let him wage a constant fight against the inherited tendencies, the corruptive instincts, the fluctuating fashions, the false pretences of the society in which he lives and moves.[18]

... these resolutions, backed by the creative energy inherent in the power of the Word of God ...[19]

... in the heart of society itself ... the ominous signs of increasing extravagance and profligacy are but lending fresh impetus to the forces of revolt and reaction that are growing more distinct every day ...[20]

Let us take heart therefore, and labour with renewed vigour and deepened understanding to contribute our share to those forces which, whether or not cognizant of the regenerating Faith of Bahá'u'lláh in this age, are operating, each in its respective sphere and under His all-encompassing guidance, for the uplift and the salvation of humanity.[21]

From Persia, the cradle of our Faith and the object of our tenderest affections, there breaks upon us the news of the first stirrings of that social and political Reformation which, as we firmly believe, is but the direct and unavoidable consequence of that great spiritual Revival ushered in by the Revelation of Bahá'u'lláh. These social and political forces now released by the Source of such a tremendous Revival are bound in their turn to demolish one by one the barriers that have so long impeded its flow, sapped its vitality and obscured its radiance.[22]

... the spiritual forces centring in, and radiating from, the first Ma<u>sh</u>riqu'l-A<u>dh</u>kár in the West ...

The higher the degree of our renunciation and self-sacrifice, the wider the range of the contributing believers, the more apparent will become the vitalizing forces that are to emanate from this unique and sacred Edifice ...[23]

Theirs will be the conviction that an all-loving and ever-watchful Father Who, in the past, and at various stages in the evolution of mankind, has sent forth His Prophets as the Bearers of His Message and the Manifestations of His Light to mankind, cannot at this critical period of their civilization withhold from His children the Guidance which they sorely need amid the darkness which has beset them, and which neither the light of science nor that of human intellect and wisdom can succeed in dissipating ... Nothing short of direct and constant interaction between the spiritual forces emanating from this House of Worship centring in the heart of the Ma<u>sh</u>riqu'l-A<u>dh</u>kár, and the energies consciously displayed by those who administer its affairs in their service to humanity can possibly provide the necessary agency capable of removing the ills that have so long and so grievously afflicted humanity.[24]

We have only to refer to the warnings uttered by 'Abdu'l-Bahá in order to realize the extent and character of the forces that are destined to contest with God's holy Faith ...

Stupendous as is the struggle which His words foreshadow, they also testify to the complete victory which the upholders of the Greatest Name are destined eventually to achieve.[25]

Few will fail to recognize that the Spirit breathed by Bahá'u'lláh upon the world, and which is manifesting itself with varying degrees of intensity through the efforts consciously displayed by His avowed supporters and indirectly through certain humanitarian organizations, can never permeate and exercise an abiding influence upon mankind unless and until it incarnates itself in a visible Order, which would bear His name, wholly identify itself with His principles, and function in conformity with His laws.[26]

He hopes that you will stand firm, unaffected by the dark forces around us, and that you will help to carry the message of Bahá'u'lláh far and wide.[27]

Might it not happen . . . that out of this world eruption there may stream forces of such spiritual energy as shall recall, nay eclipse, the splendour of those signs and wonders that accompanied the establishment of the Faith of Jesus Christ? Might there not emerge out of the agony of a shaken world a religious revival of such scope and power as to even transcend the potency of those world-directing forces with which the Religions of the Past have, at fixed intervals and according to an inscrutable Wisdom, revived the fortunes of declining ages and peoples?[28]

. . . that nothing short of a power that is born of God can succeed in establishing it [the Oneness of Mankind].[29]

That the forces of a world catastrophe can alone precipitate such a new phase of human thought is, alas, becoming increasingly apparent. That nothing short of the fire of a severe ordeal, unparalleled in its intensity, can fuse and weld the discordant entities that constitute the elements of present-day civilization, into the integral components of the world commonwealth of the future, is a truth which future events will increasingly demonstrate.[30]

Uttered at a time when its possibility had not yet been seriously envisaged in any part of the world, it has, by virtue of that celestial potency which the Spirit of Bahá'u'lláh has breathed into it, come at last to be regarded, by an increasing number of thoughtful men, not only as an approaching possibility, but as the necessary outcome of the forces now operating in the world.[31]

The primary consideration is the Spirit that has to permeate our economic life and this will gradually crystallize itself into definite institutions and principles that will help to bring about the ideal conditions foretold by Bahá'u'lláh.[32]

They should therefore open their eyes to the existing conditions, study the evil forces that are at play and then with a concerted effort arise and bring about the necessary reforms – reforms that shall contain within their scope the spiritual as well as social and political phases of human life.[33]

. . . evidence of the invincible power with which the Almighty has chosen to invest it from the moment of its inception.

That the Cause associated with the name of Bahá'u'lláh feeds itself upon those hidden springs of celestial strength which no force of human personality, whatever its glamour, can replace . . .[34]

Springing from a finite mind, begotten of human fancy, and oftentimes the product of ill-conceived designs, such movements succeed, by reason of their novelty, their appeal to man's baser instincts and their dependence upon the resources of a sordid world, in dazzling for a time the eyes of men, only to plunge finally from the heights of their meteoric career into the darkness of oblivion, dissolved by the very forces that had assisted in their creation.[35]

. . . the very operation of the world-unifying forces that are at work in this age . . .[36]

Difficult and delicate though be our task, the sustaining power of Bahá'u'lláh and of His Divine guidance will assuredly assist us if we follow steadfastly in His way, and strive to uphold the integrity of His laws. The light of His redeeming grace, which no earthly power can obscure, will if we persevere, illuminate our path, as we steer our course amid the snares and pitfalls of a troubled age, and will enable us to discharge our duties in a manner that would redound to the glory and honour of His blessed Name.[37]

Shoghi Effendi's earnest hope and plea is, therefore, that we who have been chosen to act as the dawn-breakers of a new era may not sit idly and leave the world enveloped in its social and spiritual darkness; that we may arise, and, lifting high the torch of guidance, bring light and hope to the heart of a perishing humanity.[38]

And these forces of darkness are leading humanity to absolute destruction. This state of affairs will continue until the world is awakened to the importance of the Message of Bahá'u'lláh – a Message especially sent by God to heal human ills in this present day.[39]

... the powers latent in this sacred Faith.[40]

Its past history, stained by the blood of countless martyrs, may well inspire us with the thought that, whatever may yet befall this Cause, however formidable the forces that may still assail it, however numerous the reverses it will inevitably suffer, its onward march can never be stayed, and that it will continue to advance until the very last promise, enshrined within the words of Bahá'u'lláh, shall have been completely redeemed.[41]

We cannot segregate the human heart from the environment outside us and say that once one of these is reformed everything will be improved. Man is organic with the world. His inner life moulds the environment and is itself also deeply affected by it. The one acts upon the other and every abiding change in the life of man is the result of these mutual reactions.

No movement in the world directs its attention upon both these aspects of human life and has full measures for their improvement, save the teachings of Bahá'u'lláh. And this is its distinctive feature. If we desire therefore the good of the world we should strive to spread those teaching and also practise them in our own life. Through them will the human heart be changed, and also our social environment provides the atmosphere in which we can grow spiritually and reflect in full the light of God shining through the revelation of Bahá'u'lláh.[42]

... the rapid progress of the Faith means the hastening of the final victory of goodness over the dark forces of evil that are at present threatening the world.[43]

No true and faithful Bahá'í should in this day remain idle or seek what would give him comfort or even inner satisfaction. We should be constantly assailing the forces of darkness that have enveloped the earth and hasten the dawn of the new day foretold by Bahá'u'lláh.[44]

TO ITS DELEGATES [1937 American Convention] GIVEN GREAT OPPORTUNITY RELEASE FORCES WHICH WILL USHER IN ERA WHOSE SPLENDOUR MUST OUTSHINE HEROIC AGE OUR BELOVED CAUSE . . .[45]

May the Beloved speedily and completely release you from the dark forces which have assailed you and enable you to triumph over all obstacles and thus serve effectively His Faith.[46]

He is firmly convinced that through perseverance and concerted action the cause of Peace will eventually triumph over all the dark forces which threaten the welfare and progress of the world today.[47]

KEITH'S PRECIOUS LIFE OFFERED UP IN SACRIFICE TO BELOVED CAUSE IN BAHÁ'U'LLÁH'S NATIVE LAND. ON PERSIAN SOIL FOR PERSIA'S SAKE, SHE ENCOUNTERED, CHALLENGED AND FOUGHT THE FORCES OF DARKNESS WITH HIGH DISTINCTION, INDOMITABLE WILL, UNSWERVING, EXEMPLARY LOYALTY.[48]

For more than one year she toiled and suffered, undismayed by the forces of darkness which so increasingly challenge the devotion and loyalty, and hamper the progress of the work, of our Persian brethren.[49]

Whatever our shortcomings may be, and however formidable the forces of darkness which besiege us today, the unification of mankind as outlined and ensured by the World Order of Bahá'u'lláh will in the fullness of time be firmly and permanently established.[50]

The onrushing forces so miraculously released through the agency of two independent and swiftly successive Manifestations are now under our very eyes and through the care of the chosen stewards of a far-flung Faith being gradually mustered and disciplined. They are slowly crystallizing into institutions that will come to be regarded as the hall-mark and glory of the age we are called upon to establish and by our deeds immortalize.[51]

. . . with which He Who is the vehicle of so mysterious an energy must needs be invested.[52]

The potent energies released through the ascension of the Centre of His Covenant crystallized into this supreme, this infallible Organ for the accomplishment of a Divine Purpose. The Will and Testament of 'Abdu'l-Bahá unveiled its character, reaffirmed its basis, supplemented its principles, asserted its indispensability, and enumerated its chief institutions.[53]

The creative energies released by the Law of Bahá'u'lláh, permeating and evolving within the mind of 'Abdu'l-Bahá, have, by their very impact and close interaction, given birth to an Instrument [the Will and Testament of 'Abdu'l-Bahá] which may be viewed as the Charter of the New World Order which is at once the glory and the promise of this most great Dispensation.[54]

To what else if not to the power and majesty which this Administrative Order – the rudiments of the future all-enfolding Bahá'í Commonwealth – is destined to manifest, can these utterances of Bahá'u'lláh allude: 'The world's equilibrium hath been upset through the vibrating influence of this most great, this new World Order. Mankind's ordered life hath been revolutionized through the agency of this unique, this wondrous System – the like of which mortal eyes have never witnessed.'[55]

He wishes you to persevere in your efforts and not be disheartened by the forces of darkness assailing you on every side. By the power of action and prayer, he feels certain, you will be able to overcome them all.[56]

Nothing short of this Divine spirit, as expressed through the self-sacrificing and confident labours of the . . . friends, could have so effectively subdued those forces which every now and then threatened to undermine the foundations of your Assembly, and thus overthrow the entire system of the Administration in your land.[57]

FORCES WHICH PROGRESSIVE REVELATION OF THIS MIGHTY SYMBOL OF OUR FAITH IS FAST RELEASING IN HEART OF A SORELY TRIED CONTINENT NO ONE OF THIS GENERATION CAN CORRECTLY APPRAISE. A NEW HOUR HAS STRUCK IN HISTORY OUR BELOVED CAUSE CALLING FOR NATION-WIDE, SYSTEMATIC, SUSTAINED EFFORTS IN TEACHING FIELD, ENABLING THEREBY THESE FORCES TO BE DIRECTED INTO SUCH CHANNELS AS SHALL REDOUND TO GLORY OF OUR FAITH AND HONOUR OF ITS INSTITU-TIONS.[58]

The Faith of Bahá'u'lláh constitutes, indeed, the stage of maturity in the development of mankind. His appearance has released such spiritual forces which will continue to animate, for many long years to come, the world in its development.[59]

. . . an effort [in teaching activity] unexampled in its scope and sustained vitality is urgently required so that the moving spirit of its Founder may permeate and transform the lives of the countless multitudes that hunger for its teachings.[60]

. . . the degree to which its moving Spirit has shown itself capable of assimilating the diversified elements within its pale, of cleansing them of all forms of prejudice and of fusing them with its own structure . . .[61]

Though the Heroic Age of His Faith is passed, the creative energies which that Age has released have not as yet crystallized into that world society which, in the fullness of time, is to mirror forth the brightness of His glory . . . We may well believe, we who are called upon to experience the operation of the dark forces destined to unloose a flood of agonizing afflictions, that the darkest hour that must precede the dawn of the Golden Age of our Faith has not yet struck.[62]

As we view the world around us, we are compelled to observe the manifold evidences of that universal fermentation which, in every continent of the globe and in every department of human life, be it religious, social, economic or political, is purging and reshaping humanity in anticipation of the Day when the wholeness of the human race will have been recognized and its unity established. A twofold process, however, can be distinguished, each tending, in its own way and with an accelerated momentum, to bring to a climax the forces that are transforming the face of our planet. The first is essentially an integrating process, while the second is fundamentally disruptive. The former, as it steadily evolves, unfolds a System which may well serve as a pattern for that world polity towards which a strangely-disordered world is continually advancing; while the latter, as its disintegrating influence deepens, tends to tear down, with increasing violence, the antiquated barriers that seek to block humanity's progress towards its destined goal. The constructive process stands associated with the nascent Faith of Bahá'u'lláh, and is the harbinger of the New World Order that Faith must erelong establish. The destructive forces that characterize the other should be identified with a civilization that has refused to answer to the expectation of a new age, and is consequently falling into chaos and decline.

A titanic, a spiritual struggle, unparalleled in its magnitude yet unspeakably glorious in its ultimate consequences, is being waged as a result of these opposing tendencies, in this age of transition through which the organized community of the followers of Bahá'u'lláh and mankind as a whole are passing.

The Spirit that has incarnated itself in the institutions of a rising Faith has, in the course of its onward march for the redemption of the world, encountered and is now battling with such forces as are, in most instances, the very negation of that Spirit, and whose continued existence must inevitably hinder it from achieving its purpose. The hollow and outworn institutions, the obsolescent doctrines and beliefs, the effete and discredited traditions which these forces represent, it should be observed, have, in certain instances, been undermined by virtue of their senility, the loss of their cohesive power, and their own inherent corruption. A few have been swept away by the onrushing forces which the Bahá'í Faith has, at the hour of its birth, so mysteriously released. Others, as a direct result of a vain and feeble resistance to its rise in the initial stages of its development, have died out and been utterly discredited. Still others, fearful of the pervasive influence of the institutions in which that same Spirit had, at a later stage, been embodied, had mobilized their forces and launched their attack, destined to sustain, in their turn, after a brief and illusory success, an ignominious defeat.[63]

The whole world, wherever and however we survey it, offers us the sad and pitiful spectacle of a vast, an enfeebled, and moribund organism, which is being torn politically and strangulated economically by forces it has ceased to either control or comprehend.[64]

Would it be untrue to maintain that in a world of unsettled faith and disturbed thought, a world of steadily mounting armaments, of unquenchable hatred and rivalries, the progress, however fitful, of the forces working in harmony with the spirit of the age can already be discerned?[65]

. . . this healing Agency, this leavening Power, this cementing Force, intensely alive and all-pervasive, has been taking shape, is crystallizing into institutions, is mobilizing its forces, and is preparing for the spiritual conquest and the complete redemption of mankind.[66]

Numerous and powerful have been the forces that have schemed, both from within and from without, in lands both far and near, to quench its light and abolish its holy name.[67]

. . . confident in the society-building power which their Faith possesses . . .[68]

The Faith of Bahá'u'lláh has assimilated, by virtue of its creative, its regulative and ennobling energies, the varied races, nationalities, creeds and classes that have sought its shadow, and have pledged unswerving fealty to its cause.[69]

The whole of mankind is groaning, is dying to be led to unity, and to terminate its age-long martyrdom. And yet it stubbornly refuses to embrace the light and acknowledge the sovereign authority of the one Power that can extricate it from its entanglements, and avert the woeful calamity that threatens to engulf it.[70]

[humanity is] . . . impelled by the unifying forces of life . . . [towards the goal of a world federal system].[71]

Who can visualize the realms which the human spirit, vitalized by the outpouring light of Bahá'u'lláh, shining in the plenitude of its glory, will discover?[72]

As the proclamation of the Message reverberates throughout the land, as its resistless march gathers momentum, as the field of its operation widens and the numbers of its upholders and champions multiply, its potentialities will correspondingly unfold, exerting a most beneficial influence, not only on every community throughout the Bahá'í world, but on the immediate fortunes of a travailing society . . . The Faith of God is gaining in stature, effectiveness and power.[73]

For Bahá'u'lláh has promised His Divine assistance to every one who arises with a pure and detached heart to spread His Holy Word, even though he may be bereft of every human knowledge and capacity, and notwithstanding the forces of darkness and of opposition which may be arrayed against him.[74]

The twofold task they have arisen to perform will, if carried out in time, release the potentialities with which the community of the Greatest Name has been so generously and mysteriously endowed by 'Abdu'l-Bahá.[75]

The Bahá'í teacher must be all confidence. Therein lies his strength and the secret of his success. Though single-handed, and no matter how great the apathy of the people around you may be, you should have faith that the hosts of the Kingdom are on your side, and that through their help you are bound to overcome the forces of darkness that are facing the Cause of God.[76]

To such a priceless privilege the inheritors of the shining grace of Bahá'u'lláh cannot surely be indifferent.[77]

May the all-conquering Spirit of Bahá'u'lláh be so infused into each component part of this harmoniously functioning System as to enable it to contribute its proper share to the consummation of the Plan.[78]

. . . as the impelling forces which have set in motion this mighty undertaking [the Seven Year Plan] acquire added momentum and its potentialities are more fully manifested, they who are responsible for its success . . . must evince a more burning enthusiasm . . .[79]

He wishes me to urge you not to feel disturbed by the dreams you have had, but rather to make every effort to resist and overcome the forces of darkness that assail your mind.[80]

Then and only then will this tender sapling, embedded in the fertile soil of a Divinely appointed Administrative Order, and energized by the dynamic processes of its institutions, yield its richest and destined fruit.[81]

. . . IN THESE DAYS WHEN SINISTER UNCONTROLLABLE FORCES ARE DEEPENING CLEAVAGE SUNDERING PEOPLES NATIONS CREEDS CLASSES . . .[82]

The Guardian too will specially and earnestly pray on your behalf, that your heart may be comforted and cheered, and may be set free from the forces of darkness that so strongly assail it.[83]

Regarding your questions relative to the condition of those people who are described in the Gospel as being possessed of devils; this should be interpreted figuratively; devil or satan is symbolic of evil and dark forces yielding to temptation.[84]

. . . the dynamic energy which animates the stalwart pioneers of the World Order of Bahá'u'lláh . . .[85]

Such close interaction, such complete cohesion, such continual harmony and fellowship between the various agencies that contribute to the organic life, and constitute the basic framework, of every properly functioning Bahá'í community, is a phenomenon which offers a striking contrast to the disruptive tendencies which the discordant elements of present-day society so tragically manifest. Whereas every apparent trial with which the unfathomable wisdom of the Almighty deems it necessary to afflict His chosen community serves only to demonstrate afresh its essential solidarity and to consolidate its inward strength, each of the successive crises in the fortunes of a decadent age exposes more convincingly than the one preceding it the corrosive influences that are fast sapping the vitality and undermining the basis of its declining institutions.

For such demonstrations of the interpositions of an ever-watchful Providence they who stand identified with the Community of the Most Great Name must feel eternally grateful. From every fresh token of His unfailing blessing on the one hand, and of His visitation on the other, they cannot but derive immense hope and courage. Alert to seize every opportunity which the revolutions of the wheel of destiny within their Faith offers them, and undismayed by the prospect of spasmodic convulsions that must sooner or later fatally affect those who have refused to embrace its light, they, and those who will labour after them, must press forward until the processes now set in motion will have each spent its force and contributed its share towards the birth of the Order now stirring in the womb of a travailing age.

These recurrent crises which, with ominous frequency and resistless force, are afflicting an ever-increasing portion of the human race must of necessity continue, however impermanently, to exercise, in a certain measure, their baleful influence upon a world community which has spread its ramifications to the uttermost ends of the earth. How can the beginnings of a world upheaval, unleashing forces that are so gravely deranging the social, the religious, the political, and the economic equilibrium of organized society, throwing into chaos and confusion political systems, racial doctrines, social conceptions, cultural standards, religious associations, and trade relationships – how can such agitations, on a scale so vast, so unprecedented, fail to produce any repercussions on the institutions of a Faith of such tender age whose teachings have a direct and vital bearing on each of these spheres of human life and conduct?

Little wonder, therefore, if they who are holding aloft the banner of so pervasive a Faith, so challenging a Cause, find themselves affected by the impact of these world-shaking forces. Little wonder if they find that in the midst of this whirlpool of contending passions their freedom has been curtailed, their tenets contemned, their institutions assaulted, their motives maligned, their authority jeopardized, their claim rejected.[86]

. . . yet the Force which energizes your mission is limitless in its range and incalculable in its potency.[87]

. . . the saving grace and the energizing influence of their Revelation.[88]

For it is precisely under such circumstances, and by such means that the Prophets have, from time immemorial, chosen and were able to demonstrate their redemptive power to raise from the depths of abasement and of misery, the people of their own race and nation, empowering them to transmit in turn to other races and nations the saving grace and the energizing influence of their Revelation.[89]

It is precisely by reason of the patent evils which, notwithstanding its other admittedly great characteristics and achievements, an excessive and binding materialism has unfortunately engendered within it that the Author of their Faith and the Centre of His Covenant have singled it [the American Bahá'í community] out to become the standard-bearer of the New World Order envisioned in their writings. It is by such means as this that Bahá'u'lláh can best demonstrate to a heedless generation His almighty power to raise up from the very midst of a people, immersed in a sea of materialism, a prey to one of the most virulent and long-standing forms of racial prejudice, and notorious for its political corruption, lawlessness and laxity in moral standards, men and women who, as time goes by, will increasingly exemplify those essential virtues of self-renunciation, of moral rectitude, of chastity, of indiscriminating fellowship, of holy discipline, and of spiritual insight that will fit them for the preponderating share they will have in calling into being that World Order and that World Civilization of which their country, no less than the entire human race, stands in desperate need.[90]

A rectitude of conduct, an abiding sense of undeviating justice, unobscured by the demoralizing influences which a corruption-ridden political life so strikingly manifests; a chaste, pure, and holy life, unsullied and unclouded by the indecencies, the vices, the false standards, which an inherently deficient moral code tolerates, perpetuates, and fosters; a fraternity freed from the cancerous growth of racial prejudice, which is eating into the vitals of an already debilitated society – these are the ideals which the American believers must, from now on, individually and through concerted action, strive to promote . . . ideals which are the chief propelling forces that can most effectively accelerate the march of their institutions, plans, and enterprises, that can guard the honour and integrity of their Faith, and subdue any obstacles that may confront it in the future.[91]

That God-born Force, irresistible in its sweeping power, incalculable in its potency, unpredictable in its course, mysterious in its working, and awe-inspiring in its manifestations – a Force which, as the Báb has written, 'vibrates within the innermost being of all created things', and which, according to Bahá'u'lláh, has through its 'vibrating influence', 'upset the equilibrium of the world and revolutionized its ordered life' – such a Force, acting even as a two-edged sword, is, under our very eyes, sundering, on the one hand, the age-old ties which for centuries have held together the fabric of civilized society, and is unloosing, on the other, the bonds that still fetter the infant and as yet unemancipated Faith of Bahá'u'lláh. The undreamt-of opportunities offered through the operation of this Force – the American believers must now rise, and fully and courageously exploit them . . .

A world, dimmed by the steadily dying-out light of religion, heaving with the explosive forces of a blind and triumphant nationalism; scorched with the fires of pitiless persecution, whether racial or religious; deluded by the false theories and doctrines that threaten to supplant the worship of God and the sanctification of His laws; enervated by a rampant and brutal materialism; disintegrating through the corrosive influence of moral and spiritual decadence; and enmeshed in the coils of economic anarchy and strife – such is the spectacle presented to men's eyes, as a result of the sweeping changes which this revolutionizing Force, as yet in the initial stage of its operation, is now producing in the life of the entire planet.

So sad and moving a spectacle, bewildering as it must be to every observer unaware of the purposes, the prophecies, and promises of

Bahá'u'lláh, far from casting dismay into the hearts of His followers, or paralysing their efforts, cannot but deepen their faith, and excite their enthusiastic eagerness to arise and display, in the vast field traced for them by the pen of 'Abdu'l-Bahá, their capacity to play their part in the work of universal redemption proclaimed by Bahá'u'lláh.[92]

So powerful will be the effusions of Divine grace . . . that its members will find themselves overpowered by the evidences of their regenerative power.[93]

. . . launch an offensive against the powers of darkness, of corruption, and of ignorance, an offensive that must extend to the uttermost end of the Southern continent . . .[94]

The creative energies, mysteriously generated by the first stirrings of the embryonic World Order of Bahá'u'lláh, have, as soon as released within a nation destined to become its cradle and champion, endowed that nation with the worthiness, and invested it with the powers and capacities, and equipped it spiritually, to play the part foreshadowed in these prophetic words. The potencies which this God-given mission has infused into its people are, on the one hand, beginning to be manifested through the conscious efforts and the nationwide accomplishments, in both the teaching and administrative spheres of Bahá'í activity, of the organized community of the followers of Bahá'u'lláh in the North American continent. These same potencies, apart from, yet collateral with these efforts and accomplishments, are, on the other hand, insensibly shaping, under the impact of the world political and economic forces, the destiny of that nation, and are influencing the lives and actions of both its government and its people.[95]

For no matter how ignorant of the Source from which those directing energies proceed, and however slow and laborious the process, it is becoming increasingly evident that the nation as a whole, whether through the agency of its government or otherwise, is gravitating, under the influence of forces that it can neither comprehend nor control, towards such associations and policies, wherein, as indicated by 'Abdu'l-Bahá, her true destiny must lie. Both the community of the American believers, who are aware of that Source, and the great mass of their countrymen, who have not as yet recognized the Hand that directs their destiny, are contributing, each in its own way, to the realization of the hopes, and the fulfilment of the promises, voiced in the above-quoted words of 'Abdu'l-Bahá.[96]

As the days roll by, as the perturbations of an imperiled civilization are more alarmingly manifested, the potentialities of God's creative Plan correspondingly unfold, and the valour and heroism of its intrepid supporters are more widely and convincingly demonstrated.[97]

UPSURGE OF BAHÁ'U'LLÁH'S IMPELLING SPIRIT CANNOT WILL NOT BE STEMMED IMPEDED.[98]

. . . POWERS RELEASED [FOR] CONTEMPLATED CAMPAIGN.[99]

The latter is essentially pioneer in nature, demanding first and foremost those qualities of renunciation, tenacity, dauntlessness and passionate fervour that can alone brave the dangers and sweep away the obstacles with which an infant Faith, struggling against vested interests and face to face with the entrenched forces of prejudice, of ignorance and fanaticism, must needs contend.[100]

Slowly and patiently they [Bahá'í administrators] are canalizing the spirit that at once directs, energizes and safeguards its [the structural machinery of the Faith] operation.[101]

The spiritual forces mysteriously released are already operating with increasing momentum, unchallenged and unchecked.[102]

The friends . . . should not feel bewildered, for they have the assurance of Bahá'u'lláh that whatever the nature and character of the forces of opposition facing the Cause, its eventual triumph is indubitably certain.[103]

The assurance that in this gloomy hour when the whole world is being shaken by the forces of darkness, and humanity at large is beginning to experience the fire of that ordeal foretold by Bahá'u'lláh, the friends are more than ever closely united with him in true bonds of spiritual fellow-ship is indeed the source of deepest comfort to him . . .[104]

Evil forces do take control of our life, but it is within our power to free ourselves from falling under their subjection.[105]

. . . evidences of the animating Force that propels the Plan towards its final consummation.

Varied and abundant as have been the past manifestations of this driving, resistless Force, they cannot but pale before the brilliant victories which its progressive and systematic development must achieve in the future.[106]

As the administrative processes expand, as their operation steadily improves, as their necessity is more fully and strikingly demonstrated, and their beneficent influence correspondingly grows more apparent and evident, so will the blessings, the strength, and guidance bestowed by Him Who animates and directs these processes be more abundantly vouchsafed to those who have been called upon to utilize them, in this age, for the execution of God's Purpose and for the ultimate redemption of a sore-stricken, travailing humanity. Many will be the setbacks, the shocks and the disturbances, which the commotions of a convulsive age must produce; yet no force, however violent and worldwide in its range and catastrophic in its immediate consequences, can either halt these processes or deflect their appointed course.[107]

DISRUPTIVE FORCES ASSOCIATED HUMANITY'S WORLD-SHAKING ORDEAL CLOSELY INTERRELATED CONSTRUCTIVE POTENTIALITIES INHERENT AMERICAN BELIEVERS DIVINELY-ORDAINED PLAN. BOTH DIRECTLY HASTENING EMERGENCE SPIRITUAL WORLD ORDER STIRRING WOMB TRA-VAILING AGE.[108]

A tempest, unprecedented in its violence, unpredictable in its course, catastrophic in its immediate effects, unimaginably glorious in its ultimate consequences, is at present sweeping the face of the earth. Its driving power is remorselessly gaining in range and momentum. Its cleansing force, however much undetected, is increasing with every passing day.

Humanity, gripped in the clutches of its devastating power, is smitten by the evidences of its resistless fury. It can neither perceive its origin, nor probe its significance, nor discern its outcome. Bewildered, agonized and helpless, it watches this great and mighty wind of God invading the remotest and fairest regions of the earth, rocking its foundations, deranging its equilibrium, sundering its nations, disrupting the homes of its peoples, wasting its cities, driving into exile its kings, pulling down its bulwarks, uprooting its institutions, dimming its light, and harrowing up the souls of its inhabitants.[109]

Which one of the multitudes of creeds, sects, races, parties and classes and of the highly diversified schools of human thought, considered it necessary to direct its gaze towards the rising light of the Faith, to contemplate its unfolding system, to ponder its hidden processes, to appraise its weighty message, to acknowledge its regenerative power, to embrace its salutary truth, or to proclaim its eternal verities?[110]

... spiritual, revolutionary forces which, synchronizing with the first dawnings of the World Order of His Faith, are upsetting the equilibrium, and throwing into such confusion, the ancient institutions of mankind.[111]

Aided by the forces which the Communist movement has unloosed, reinforced by the political consequences of the last war, accelerated by the excessive, the blind, the intolerant, and militant nationalism which is now convulsing the nations, and stimulated by the rising tide of materialism, irreligion, and paganism, this process is not only tending to subvert ecclesiastical institutions, but appears to be leading to the rapid dechristianization of the masses in many Christian countries.[112]

It is the creative energies which His Revelation has released in the 'year sixty', and later reinforced by the successive effusions of celestial power vouchsafed in the 'year nine' and the 'year eighty' to all mankind, that have instilled into humanity the capacity to attain this final stage in its organic and collective evolution.[113]

The Revelation of Bahá'u'lláh has, in His own words, 'lent a fresh impulse and set a new direction' to this vast process now operating in the world.

The fires lit by this great ordeal are the consequence of men's failure to recognize it.[114]

Ours rather the duty . . . to lend our share of assistance, in whichever way circumstances may enable us, to the operation of the forces which, as marshalled and directed by Bahá'u'lláh, are leading humanity out of the valley of misery and shame to the loftiest summits of power and glory.[115]

In these days when the forces of inharmony and disunity are rampant throughout the world, the Bahá'ís must cling to their Faith and to each other and, in spite of every difficulty and suffering, protect the unity of the Cause.[116]

The Faith of Bahá'u'lláh – that priceless gem of Divine Revelation, enshrining the Spirit of God and incarnating His Purpose for mankind in this age – can neither aspire nor expect to escape unhurt amid the hurricane of human disasters that blows around it. By most men unnoticed, scorned and ridiculed by some, feared and challenged by others, this world-redemptive Faith, for whose precious sake the world is undergoing such agonies, finds its virgin strength assailed, and its infant institutions hemmed in by the dark forces which a godless civilization has unloosed over the face of the planet.[117]

The Plan itself, propelled by the energies released by those immortal Tablets which constitute its charter . . .[118]

AS ARENA WORLD-CONVULSING CONTEST BROADENS, AS WOUNDS IT INFLICTS DEEPEN, AS ISSUES IT RAISES AGGRAVATE MULTIPLY SO WILL OPERATION OF THE SPIRITUAL FORCES DESTINED CAST BURDEN TRAVAILING AGE BE ACCELERATED.[119]

Generated by the propelling and purifying forces of a mysterious Faith, born of delusion or malice, winning a fleeting notoriety derived from the precarious advantages of wealth, fame, or fortune, these movements sponsored by deluded, self-seeking adventurers find themselves, sooner or later, enmeshed in the machinations of their authors, are buried in shame, and sink eventually into complete oblivion.[120]

. . . this increased hostility being accompanied by a still more arresting revelation of Divine Power and a more abundant effusion of celestial grace, which, by enabling the upholders of that Faith to register still more brilliant victories, would thereby generate issues of still more vital import . . .

The resistless march of the Faith of Bahá'u'lláh, viewed in this light, and propelled by the stimulating influences which the unwisdom of its enemies and the force latent within itself both engender, resolves itself into a series of rhythmic pulsations, precipitated, on the one hand, through the explosive outbursts of its foes, and the vibrations of Divine Power, on the other, which speed it, with ever-increasing momentum, along that predestined course traced for it by the Hand of the Almighty.

As opposition to the Faith, from whatever source it may spring, whatever form it may assume, however violent its outbursts, is admittedly the motive-power that galvanizes, on the one hand, the souls of its valiant defenders, and taps for them, on the other, fresh springs of that Divine and inexhaustible Energy, we, who are called upon to represent, defend and promote its interests, should, far from regarding any manifestation of hostility as an evidence of the weakening of the pillars of the Faith, acclaim it as both a God-sent gift and a God-sent opportunity . . .[121]

. . . that Formative Period which is to witness the gradual crystallization of those creative energies which the Faith has released, and the consequent emergence of that World Order for which those forces were made to operate.

Fierce and relentless will be the opposition which this crystallization and emergence must provoke.[122]

The believers must realize that the forces of prejudice are, along with so many other evil practices, growing at present stronger in the darkness surrounding humanity.[123]

If we could perceive the true reality of things we would see that the greatest of all battles raging in the world today is the spiritual battle. If the believers like yourself, young and eager and full of life, desire to win laurels for true and undying heroism, then let them join in the spiritual battle – whatever their physical occupation may be – which involves the very soul of man. The hardest and the noblest task in the world today is to be a true Bahá'í; this requires that we defeat not only the current evils prevailing all over the world, but the weaknesses, attachments to the past, prejudices, and selfishnesses that may be inherited and acquired within our own characters; that we give forth a shining and incorruptible example to our fellow-men.[124]

The completion of the Temple should . . . release tremendous and unprecedented forces of spiritual energy destined to be wholly consecrated to the teaching tasks . . .[125]

The Cause of God is endowed with tremendous powers, and the reason the believers do not gain more from it is because they have not learned to fully draw on these mighty forces of love and strength and harmony generated by the Faith.[126]

The creative energies its completion [the American House of Worship] must unleash are incalculable.[127]

You should never allow the many dark thoughts and dark forces in the world today to weigh on your mind or depress you. The world is very black at present, and humanity in a very degraded condition spiritually. We must accept this fact, but not allow it to influence us. Our life is in the Cause of God, and we draw our strength from it, and the world of the Cause is a world of light.[128]

The weight of the potentialities with which this Faith . . . has been endowed, staggers our imagination . . .
Already in the space of less than a century the operation of the mysterious processes generated by its creative spirit has provoked a tumult in human society such as no mind can fathom. Itself undergoing a period of incubation during its primitive age, it has, through the emergence of its slowly-crystallizing system, induced a fermentation in the general life of mankind designed to shake the very foundations of a disordered society, to purify its life-blood, to reorientate and reconstruct its institutions, and shape its final destiny.
To what else can the observant eye or the unprejudiced mind, acquainted with the signs and portents heralding the birth, and accom-

panying the rise, of the Faith of Bahá'u'lláh ascribe this dire, this planetary upheaval, with its attendant destruction, misery and fear, if not to the emergence of His embryonic World Order, which, as He Himself has unequivocally proclaimed, has 'deranged the equilibrium of the world and revolutionized mankind's ordered life'? To what agency, if not to the irresistible diffusion of that world-shaking, world-energizing, world-redeeming spirit, which the Báb has affirmed is 'vibrating in the innermost realities of all created things' can the origins of this portentous crisis, incomprehensible to man, and admittedly unprecedented in the annals of the human race, be attributed?

... in these we can readily recognize the evidences of the travail of an age that has sustained the impact of His Revelation, that has ignored His summons, and is now labouring to be delivered of its burden, as a direct consequence of the impulse communicated to it by the generative, the purifying, the transmuting influence of His Spirit.[129]

... the century that has seen this Spirit burst forth upon the world, as well as the initial stages of its subsequent incarnation in a System that must evolve into an Order designed to embrace the whole of mankind, and capable of fulfilling the high destiny that awaits man on this planet.[130]

... that World Order that must incarnate the soul, execute the laws, and fulfil the purpose of the Faith of God in this day.[131]

... the Formative, the Transitional, the Iron Age which is to witness the crystallization and shaping of the creative energies released by His Revelation.[132]

The fourth period (1921–1944) is motivated by the forces radiating from the Will and Testament of 'Abdu'l-Bahá, that Charter of Bahá'u'lláh's New World Order, the offspring resulting from the mystic intercourse between Him Who is the Source of the Law of God and the mind of One Who is the vehicle and interpreter of that Law.[133]

The 'Man Child', mentioned in the Book of Revelation, destined to 'rule all nations with a rod of iron', had released, through His coming, the creative energies which, reinforced by the effusions of a swiftly succeeding and infinitely mightier Revelation, were to instil into the entire human race the capacity to achieve its organic unification, attain maturity and thereby reach the final stage in its age-long evolution.[134]

The forces of darkness, at first confined to the concerted hostility of the civil and ecclesiastical powers of S͟hí'ah Persia, gathering momentum, at a later stage, through the avowed and persistent opposition of the Caliph of Islám and the Sunní hierarchy in Turkey, and destined to culminate in the fierce antagonism of the sacerdotal orders associated with other and still more powerful religious systems, had launched their initial assault.[135]

The Báb – the Fountainhead from whence the vitalizing energies of a newborn Revelation had flowed . . .[136]

. . . a Revelation which, flowing out . . . from His travailing soul . . . and propagating itself as far as the ends of the earth, infused into the entire body of mankind its boundless potentialities, and is now under our very eyes, shaping the course of human society . . .[137]

. . . He describes, briefly and graphically, the impact of the onrushing force of the Divine Summons upon His entire being . . .[138]

. . . a period of great spiritual ferment, during which the Recipient of so weighty a Message restlessly anticipated the hour at which He could unburden His heavily laden soul, so replete with the potent energies released by God's nascent Revelation.[139]

. . . a ministry [Bahá'u'lláh's] which, by virtue of its creative power, its cleansing force, its healing influences, and the irresistible operation of the world-directing, world-shaping forces it released, stands unparalleled in the religious annals of the entire human race.[140]

. . . an imprisonment . . . immortalized, as it drew to a close, by the sudden eruption of the forces released by an overpowering, soul-revolutionizing Revelation.[141]

From it radiated, wave after wave, a power, a radiance and a glory which insensibly reanimated a languishing Faith, sorely-stricken, sinking into obscurity, threatened with oblivion. From it were diffused, day and night, and with ever-increasing energy, the first emanations of a Revelation which, in its scope, its copiousness, its driving force and the volume and variety of its literature, was destined to excel that of the Báb Himself.[142]

As the year 'eighty' steadily and inexorably approached, He Who had become the real leader of that community increasingly experienced, and progressively communicated to His future followers, the onrushing influences of its informing force.[143]

... the creative forces which ... reanimated a disintegrating community ...[144]

Indeed the tale which the subsequent decades of the century under review unfold to our eyes is but the record of the manifold evidences of the resistless operation of those creative forces which the revolution of fifty years of almost uninterrupted Revelation had released.[145]

To direct and canalize these forces let loose by this Heaven-sent process, and to insure their harmonious and continuous operation after His ascension, an instrument divinely ordained, invested with indisputable authority, organically linked with the Author of the Revelation Himself, was clearly indispensable. That instrument Bahá'u'lláh had expressly provided through the institution of the Covenant ...[146]

Its influence [the soul of Bahá'u'lláh] no longer circumscribed by any physical limitations, its radiance no longer beclouded by its human temple, that soul could henceforth energize the whole world to a degree unapproached at any stage in the course of its existence on this planet.[147]

... one of those periodic crises which, since the inception of the Faith of Bahá'u'lláh ... have been instrumental ... in releasing a further measure of its latent powers.[148]

This is the community [North American], it should be remembered, which . . . was called into being through the creative energies released by the proclamation of the Covenant of Bahá'u'lláh . . .[149]

That divinely instituted Covenant had, shortly after its inception, demonstrated beyond the shadow of a doubt its invincible strength through its decisive triumph over the dark forces which its Arch-Breaker had with such determination arrayed against it.[150]

The internecine struggle, now engulfing the generality of mankind, is increasingly assuming, in its range and ferocity, the proportions of the titanic upheaval foreshadowed as far back as seventy years ago by Bahá'u'lláh. It can be viewed in no other light except as a direct interposition by Him Who is the Ordainer of the Universe, the Judge of all men, and the Deliverer of the nations. It is the rod of both the anger of God and of His correction. The fierceness of its devastating power chastens the children of men for their refusal to acclaim the century-old Message of their promised, their Heaven-sent Redeemer. The fury of its flames, on the other hand, purges away the dross, and welds the limbs of humanity into one single organism, indivisible, purified, God-conscious and Divinely directed.[151]

The moment had now arrived for that undying, that world-vitalizing Spirit . . . to incarnate itself in institutions designed to canalize its outspreading energies and stimulate its growth.[152]

The creative energies unleashed by the Originator of the Law of God in this age gave birth, through their impact upon the mind of Him Who had been chosen as its unerring Expounder, to that Instrument [the Will and Testament of 'Abdu'l-Bahá], the vast implications of which the present generation, even after the lapse of twenty-three years, is still incapable of fully apprehending.[153]

. . . the forces released through the inception of the stupendous Plan conceived by Him could now flow unchecked . . . into channels designed to disclose to the world at large the potencies with which that Plan had been endowed.[154]

. . . the emergence of such a community, in a world steeped in prejudice, worshipping false gods, torn by intestine divisions, and blindly clinging to obsolescent doctrines and defective standards, could not but precipitate, sooner or later, crises no less grave, though less spectacular, than the persecutions which, in an earlier age, had raged around the Founders of that community and their early disciples.[155]

. . . the Holy Land, the world seat of this System, where its heart pulsates, where the dust of its Founders reposes, where the processes disclosing its purposes, energizing its life and shaping its destiny all originate . . .[156]

. . . through participation in the activities of societies, institutes and clubs animated by ideals akin to the principles of the Faith . . . through contact with statesmen, scholars, publicists, philanthropists and other leaders of public thought . . . have these signal victories been achieved . . .[157]

A process, God-impelled, endowed with measureless potentialities, mysterious in its workings, awful in the retribution meted out to every one seeking to resist its operation, infinitely rich in its promise for the regeneration and redemption of human kind, had been set in motion in Shíráz, had gained momentum successively in Ṭihrán, Baghdád, Adrianople and 'Akká, had projected itself across the seas, poured its generative influences into the West, and manifested the initial evidences of its marvellous, world-energizing force in the midst of the North American continent.[158]

The Instrument He had forged, the Covenant He had Himself instituted, had canalized, after His passing, the forces released by Him in the course of a forty-year ministry, had preserved the unity of His Faith and provided the impulse required to propel it forward to achieve its destiny.[159]

Impelled by the forces engendered by the revelation of that immortal and unique Document [the Will and Testament of 'Abdu'l-Bahá] . . .[160]

The Golden Age of the Faith itself must witness . . . the birth of a world civilization, inspired and directed by the creative energies released by Bahá'u'lláh's World Order, shining in its meridian splendour . . .[161]

There are dark forces in the world today of despair and hatred and suspicion; the believers must, as the Master said, turn their backs on these and their faces to Him, confident of His help and protection.[162]

The world is full of evil and dark forces and the friends must not permit these forces to get hold of them by thinking and feeling negatively towards each other . . .[163]

The impetus that has been given by the Manifestation of God for this Age is the sole one that can regenerate humanity, and as we Bahá'ís are the only ones yet aware of this new force in the world, our obligation towards our fellow men is tremendous and inescapable![164]

. . . when Bahá'ís permit the dark forces of the world to enter into their own relationships within the Faith they gravely jeopardize its progress . . .[165]

. . . the sustaining grace destined to be vouchsafed from on high to those who will arise to achieve that task and fulfil this need is boundless and assured. Its potency has been already fully experienced and abundantly demonstrated in the years that have witnessed the most prodigious efforts exerted by the American believers. A still more powerful display of its miraculous force can be confidently anticipated, if those who have felt its impact in the past arise to carry out, in the years that lie immediately ahead, the sublime and twofold task of the redemption of mankind and the establishment of the world sovereignty of Bahá'u'lláh.[166]

The believers, to better understand their own internal condition, should realize that the forces of darkness in the World are so prevalent and strong that their morbid and turbulent influence is felt by all. They should therefore consciously strive to be more loving, more united, more dedicated and prayerful than ever before, in order to fight against the atmosphere of present day society which is unloving, disunited, careless of right and wrong, and heedless of God.[167]

The forces which such a consummation [the successful completion of the British Six Year Plan] will release none can estimate sufficiently at present. The task is colossal, but the reinforcing power of Bahá'u'lláh, who is watching over it and is ready to bless and sustain it if its prosecutors arise to play their part, is likewise immeasurable.[168]

. . . the momentum of the mysterious forces driving it [the present phase of development] onward . . .

The impulse from which this historic world-embracing crusade . . . derives its creative power may be said to have in a sense originated with the Mandate issued by the Báb . . .

To this initial impulse given by the Herald of our Faith . . . a still greater force was communicated, and a more specific direction given, when the Author of our Faith Himself . . . addressed, in His Kitáb-i-Aqdas . . . some of the most celebrated passages of that Book to the Chief Magistrates of the entire American continent . . .

That same impulse was markedly accelerated when the Centre of the Covenant Himself, through a series of successive acts, chose to disclose, to an unprecedented extent, the character of the Mission reserved for the followers of Bahá'u'lláh in that continent . . .[169]

The second [Bahá'í] century is destined to witness a tremendous deployment and a notable consolidation of the forces working towards the worldwide development of that Order, as well as the first stirrings of that World Order, of which the present Administrative System is at once the precursor, the nucleus and pattern – an Order which, as it slowly crystallizes and radiates its benign influence over the entire planet, will proclaim at once the coming of age of the whole human race, as well as the maturity of the Faith itself, the progenitor of that Order.[170]

It is not for us . . . to seek to delineate the mysterious course which a God-given Mission, impelled by forces beyond our power to predict or appraise, may pursue.[171]

. . . He ['Abdu'l-Bahá], through the sustaining power of His spirit from on high, assisted it to erect the framework of those institutions that were to safeguard its unfoldment and canalize its energies . . .[172]

. . . forces of darkness, either from within or from without, may seek to dampen their ardour, to disrupt their unity and break their spirit . . .

None of these, however fierce, sinister or unyielding they may appear, must be allowed to deflect the protagonists of a God-impelled Plan from the course which 'Abdu'l-Bahá has chosen for them . . .[173]

FORCES MYSTERIOUSLY RELEASED DESIGNED DIRECT OPERATION STIMU-LATE PROCESSES ENSURE CONSUMMATION SECOND STAGE DIVINE PLAN INCONCEIVABLY POTENT. FULL RAPID USE THESE FORCES BY ORGANIZED COMMUNITY ALIVE SUBLIMITY MISSION IMPERATIVE.[174]

. . . SUSTAINING GRACE LORD OF HOSTS PROMISED EXECUTORS HIS MAN-DATE INDESCRIBABLY POTENT.[175]

The friends must, at all times, bear in mind that they are, in a way, like soldiers under attack. The world is at present in an exceedingly dark condition spiritually; hatred and prejudice, of every sort, are literally tearing it to pieces. We, on the other hand, are the custodians of the opposite forces, the forces of love, of unity, of peace and integration, and we must constantly be on our guard, whether as individuals or as an Assembly or Community, lest through us these destructive, negative forces enter into our midst. In other words we must beware lest the darkness of society become reflected in our acts and attitudes, perhaps all unconsciously. Love for each other, the deep sense that we are a new organism, the dawn-breakers of a New World Order, must constantly animate our Bahá'í lives, and we must pray to be protected from the contamination of society which is so diseased with prejudice.[176]

Such remarkable multiplication of dynamic institutions, such thrilling deployment of world-generating forces, North, South, East and West, endow the preeminent goal of the Second Seven Year Plan in Europe with extraordinary urgency and peculiar significance.[177]

This Primitive Age of the Bahá'í Era, unapproached in spiritual fecundity by any period associated with the mission of the Founder of any previous Dispensation, was impregnated, from its inception to its termination, with the creative energies generated through the advent of two independent Manifestations and the establishment of a Covenant unique in the spiritual annals of mankind.[178]

. . . the Plan . . . is energized by the all-compelling will of its Author [Abdu'l-Bahá] . . . it propels itself forward, driven by forces which its prosecutors can not hope to properly assess . . .[179]

The hosts on high, having sounded the signal, are impatient to rush forward, and demonstrate anew the irresistible force of their might.[180]

The ten countries . . . must each evolve into strongholds from which the dynamic energies of that Faith can be diffused to neighbouring territories . . .[181]

The initial clash between the forces of darkness and the army of light, as unnoticed as the landing, two millenniums ago, of the apostles of Christ on the southern shores of the European continent, is being registered by the denizens of the Abhá Kingdom.[182]

. . . when America will 'evolve into a centre from which waves of spiritual power will emanate . . .'[183]

For almost a hundred years now the warnings of Bahá'u'lláh have been ringing in men's ears, and we have every reason to believe terrible things may still befall mankind, if they do not listen to the Divine solution proposed by God's Manifestation for this day. In this connection he is constantly pointing out to the Bahá'ís that their direct Bahá'í work – teaching, perfecting the administration, propagating the Cause of God is *their* job and of immediate importance because, it is, so to speak, spiritually organic. What they are doing will release forces which will combat the terrible disintegration of society which we witness today in every field, political, economic or otherwise . . .[184]

A community now in the process of marshalling and directing, in such vast territories, in such outlying regions, amidst such a diversity of peoples, at so precarious a stage in the fortunes of mankind, forces of such incalculable potency, to serve purposes so meritorious and lofty, cannot afford to falter for a moment or retrace its steps on the path it now travels.[185]

As the international situation worsens, as the fortunes of mankind sink to a still lower ebb, the momentum of the Plan must be further accelerated, and the concerted exertions of the community responsible for its execution rise to still higher levels of consecration and heroism. As the fabric of present-day society heaves and cracks under the strain and stress of portentous events and calamities, as the fissures, accentuating the cleavage separating nation from nation, class from class, race from race, and creed from creed, multiply, the prosecutors of the Plan must evince a still greater cohesion in their spiritual lives and administrative activities, and demonstrate a higher standard of concerted effort, of mutual assistance, and of harmonious development in their collective enterprises.

Then, and only then, will the reaction to the stupendous forces, released through the operation of a divinely conceived, divinely impelled Plan, be made apparent . . .[186]

I feel assured that cumulative efforts of participants in emergency campaign launched by entire community will increasingly attract the promised inflowing grace of the holy Author of its destinies . . . [187]

The dark forces in the world, of disbelief and materialism, seem to certainly be engulfing humanity more and more – but of course, to our eyes, guided by the light of Bahá'u'lláh, it signifies the speeding up of a process of deterioration which alone can pave the way for the emergence of the new world He has ordained.[188]

Life is a constant struggle, not only against forces around us, but above all against our own ego . . . But it seems apparent that the great failure to respond to Bahá'u'lláh's instructions, appeals and warnings issued in the 19th century, has now sent the world along a path, or released forces, which must culminate in a still more violent upheaval and agony. The thing is out of hand, so to speak, and it is too late to avert catastrophic trials.[189]

Theirs is the privilege . . . to preside . . . over, and direct the forces generated by, the birth of an order that posterity will acclaim as both the offspring of that Faith, and the precursor of the Golden Age . . . [190]

... the continent of Asia, where the overwhelming majority of the followers of the Most Great Name, have endured such grievous afflictions, and are faced with grave peril, and are battling so heroically against the forces of darkness with which they are encompassed.[191]

... the forces He [the Báb] set in motion ...
   The creative energies released at the hour of the birth of His Revelation, endowing mankind with the potentialities of the attainment of maturity are deranging, during the present transitional age, the equilibrium of the entire planet as the inevitable prelude to the consummation in world unity of the coming of age of the human race.[192]

Lastly the Holy Seed of infinite preciousness, holding within itself incalculable potentialities representing the culmination of the centuries-old process of the evolution of humanity through the energies released by the series of progressive Revelations starting with Adam and concluded by the Revelation of the Seal of the Prophets, marked by the successive appearance of the branches, leaves, buds, blossoms and plucked, after six brief years by the hand of destiny, ground in the mill of martyrdom and oppression but yielding the oil whose first flickering light cast upon the sombre, subterranean walls of the Síyáh-Chál of Ṭihrán, whose fire gathered brilliance in Baghdád and shone in full resplendency in its crystal globe in Adrianople, whose rays warmed and illuminated the fringes of the American, European, Australian continents through the tender ministerings of the Centre of the Covenant, whose radiance is now overspreading the surface of the globe during the present Formative Age, whose full splendour is destined in the course of future millenniums to suffuse the entire planet.[193]

... firmly knit world-encompassing community ... energized through the simultaneous prosecution of specific plans conducted under the aegis of its national councils ...[194]

We know absence of light is darkness, but no one would assert darkness was not a fact. It exists even though it is only the absence of something else. So evil exists too, and we cannot close our eyes to it, even though it is a negative existence. We must seek to supplant it by good, and if we see an evil person is not influenceable by us, then we should shun his company for it is unhealthy.[195]

... confident of the irresistible and mysterious power instilled by the Hand of Providence in every agency associated with His Most Holy Name.[196]

... be spiritually welded into a unit at once dynamic and coherent, and be suffused with the creative, the directing and propelling forces proceeding from the Source of Revelation Himself, and be made ... the vehicle of His grace from on high ...[197]

We have been told over and over again in the Teachings that the forces of darkness attack Bahá'ís; and it is these forces which are seeking to disrupt your national body.[198]

Its driving force is the energizing influence generated by the Revelation heralded by the Báb and proclaimed by Bahá'u'lláh.[199]

May this Crusade ... provide, as it unfolds, an effective antidote to the baneful forces of atheism, nationalism, secularism and materialism that are tearing at the vitals of this turbulent continent [Asia] ...[200]

... a civilization destined as it unfolds to derive its initial impulse from the spirit animating the very institutions which, in their embryonic state, are now stirring in the womb of the present Formative Age of the Faith.[201]

It would be perhaps impossible to find a nation or people not in a state of crisis today. The materialism, the lack of true religion and the consequent baser forces in human nature which are being released, have brought the whole world to the brink of probably the greatest crisis it has ever faced or will have to face. The Bahá'ís are a part of the world. They too feel the great pressures which are brought to bear upon all people today, whoever and wherever they may be.[202]

... most important of all, its spiritual driving force must be constantly rein-forced through a firmer grasp by the individuals, ultimately responsible for its progress, of the distinguishing verities and fundamental purposes of their Faith, through a fuller dedication to its glorious Mission, and through a closer communion with its animating Spirit.[203]

. . . the impact of the forces released by a World Spiritual Crusade . . .[204]

EVIDENCES OF INCREASING HOSTILITY WITHOUT, PERSISTENT MACHINA-TIONS WITHIN, FORESHADOWING DIRE CONTESTS DESTINED TO RANGE THE ARMY OF LIGHT AGAINST THE FORCES OF DARKNESS, BOTH SECULAR AND RELIGIOUS, PREDICTED IN UNEQUIVOCAL LANGUAGE BY ʿABDUʾL-BAHÁ . . .[205]

It is hard for the friends to appreciate, when they are isolated in one of these goal territories, and see that they are making no progress in teaching others, are living in inhospitable climes for the most part, and are lonesome for Baháʾí companionship and activity, that they represent a force for good, that they are like a light-house of Baháʾuʾlláh shining at a strategic point and casting its beam out into the darkness.[206]

Bibliography

'Abdu'l-Bahá. *Foundations of World Unity*. Wilmette, IL: Bahá'í Publishing Trust, 1945.

— *Makátíb-i-'Abdu'l-Bahá* (Letters of 'Abdu'l-Bahá). 8 vols.: vols. 1–3 Cairo (1910–22), vols. 4–8 Tihran: Bahá'í National Publishing Trust (121–34) BE.

— *Paris Talks*. London: Bahá'í Publishing Trust, 1967.

— *The Promulgation of Universal Peace*. Wilmette, IL: Bahá'í Publishing Trust, 1982.

— *The Secret of Divine Civilization*. Wilmette, IL: Bahá'í Publishing Trust, 1990.

— *Selections from the Writings of 'Abdu'l-Bahá*. Haifa: Bahá'í World Centre, 1978.

— *Some Answered Questions*. Wilmette, IL: Bahá'í Publishing Trust, 1981.

— *Tablets of Abdul-Baha Abbas*. Chicago: Bahá'í Publishing Society; vol. 1, 1909; vol. 2, 1915; vol. 3, 1916.

— *Tablets of the Divine Plan*. Wilmette, IL: Bahá'í Publishing Trust, 1993.

Bahai Scriptures: Selections from the Utterances of Baha'u'llah and 'Abdu'l-Baha. Ed. Horace Holley. New York: J.J. Little and Ives, 1928.

Bahá'í World Faith. Wilmette, IL: Bahá'í Publishing Trust, 2nd ed. 1976.

Bahá'u'lláh. *Epistle to the Son of the Wolf*. Wilmette, IL: Bahá'í Publishing Trust, 1988.

— *Gleanings from the Writings of Bahá'u'lláh*. Wilmette, IL: Bahá'í Publishing Trust, 1983.

— *The Hidden Words*. Wilmette, IL: Bahá'í Publishing Trust, 1990.

— *The Kitáb-i-Aqdas*. Haifa: Bahá'í World Centre, 1992.

— *Kitáb-i-Íqán*. Wilmette, IL: Bahá'í Publishing Trust, 1989.

— *Prayers and Meditations*. Wilmette, IL: Bahá'í Publishing Trust, 1987.

— *The Summons of the Lord of Hosts: Tablets of Bahá'u'lláh*. Haifa: Bahá'í World Centre, 2002.

— *Tabernacle of Unity*. Haifa: Bahá'í World Centre, 2006.

— *Tablets of Bahá'u'lláh*. Wilmette, IL: Bahá'í Publishing Trust, 1988.

The Compilation of Compilations. Prepared by the Universal House of Justice 1963–1990. 2 vols. [Mona Vale NSW]: Bahá'í Publications Australia, 1991.

Ḥuqúqu'lláh: The Right of God. London: Bahá'í Books UK, 2007.

Lights of Guidance: A Bahá'í Reference File. Compiled by Helen Hornby. New Delhi: Bahá'í Publishing Trust, 5th ed. 1997.

Nabíl-i-A'ẓam. *The Dawn-Breakers: Nabíl's Narrative of the Early Days of the Bahá'í Revelation*. Wilmette, IL: Bahá'í Publishing Trust, 1970.

Ocean Research Library: Accessed at *Ocean* http://www.bahai-education.org/ocean/.

Shoghi Effendi. *The Advent of Divine Justice*. Wilmette, IL: Bahá'í Publishing Trust, 1990.

— *Bahá'í Administration*. Wilmette, IL: Bahá'í Publishing Trust, 1968.

— *The Bahá'í Faith, 1844–1952* (including supplement *Ten-Year International Bahá'í Teaching & Consolidation Plan, 1953–1963*). London: Bahá'í Publishing Trust, no date.

— *Citadel of Faith: Messages to America 1947–1957*. Wilmette, IL: Bahá'í Publishing Trust, 1965.

— *Dawn of a New Day: Messages to India 1923–1957*. New Delhi: Bahá'í Publishing Trust, 1970.

— *God Passes By*. Wilmette, IL: Bahá'í Publishing Trust, rev. ed. 1995.

— *Letters from the Guardian to Australia and New Zealand*. Sydney, Australia: Bahá'í Publishing Trust, 1970.

— *The Light of Divine Guidance: The Messages from the Guardian of the*

Bahá'í Faith to the Bahá'ís of Germany and Austria. 2 vols. Hofheim-Langenhain: Bahá'í-Verlag, 1982.

— *Messages to America.* Wilmette, IL: Bahá'í Publishing Committee, 1947.

— *Messages to the Bahá'í World.* Wilmette, IL: Bahá'í Publishing Trust, 1971.

— *The Promised Day is Come.* Wilmette, IL: Bahá'í Publishing Trust, rev. ed. 1980.

— *This Decisive Hour: Messages from Shoghi Effendi to the North American Bahá'ís, 1932–1946.* Wilmette, IL: Bahá'í Publishing Trust, 2002.

— *The Unfolding Destiny of the British Bahá'í Community: The Messages of the Guardian of the Bahá'í Faith to the Bahá'ís of the British Isles.* London: Bahá'í Publishing Trust, 1981.

— Unpublished letters of Shoghi Effendi, found in Bahá'í International Archives:
30 December 1923.
26 February 1926.
7 April 1933.

— Unpublished letters written on behalf of Shoghi Effendi, found in International Bahá'í Archives:
29 March 1932.
19 April 1933.
22 July 1933.
3 November 1933.
16 February 1934.
7 July 1938.
26 October 1938.
22 October 1939.
24 July 1943.
9 August 1944.
20 April 1948.
11 February 1952.

— *The World Order of Bahá'u'lláh.* Wilmette, IL: Bahá'í Publishing Trust, 1991.

Star of the West. rpt. Oxford: George Ronald, 1984.

The Universal House of Justice. *Individual Rights and Freedoms in the World Order of Bahá'u'lláh.* Wilmette IL: Bahá'í Publishing Trust, 1989.

— *Messages from the Universal House of Justice 1963–1986: The Third Epoch of the Formative Age.* Wilmette, IL: Bahá'í Publishing Trust, 1996.

— *A Wider Horizon: Selected Messages of the Universal House of Justice 1983–1992.* Riviera Beach, Florida: Palabra Publications, 1992.

References

1. The Nature of Spiritual Forces

1. Bahá'u'lláh, *Tablets*, p. 173.
2. The Báb, in Shoghi Effendi, *God Passes By*, p. xi.
3. Cable of Shoghi Effendi, 26 May 1955, in Shoghi Effendi, *Messages to the Bahá'í World*, p. 87.
4. Letter of Shoghi Effendi, 8 February 1934, in Shoghi Effendi, *World Order*, p. 155.
5. Shoghi Effendi, *God Passes By*, p. xi.
6. Letter of Shoghi Effendi, 21 December 1939, in Shoghi Effendi, *Messages to America*, p. 32.
7. Shoghi Effendi, *God Passes By*, p. 324.
8. Letter of Shoghi Effendi, 30 January 1938, in Shoghi Effendi, *Messages to America*, p. 12.
9. Shoghi Effendi, *Advent*, p. 46.
10. Shoghi Effendi, *God Passes By*, p. xii.
11. ibid. p. 106.
12. Letter of Shoghi Effendi, 12 August 1941, in Shoghi Effendi, *Messages to America*, p. 50.
13. Shoghi Effendi, *God Passes By*, p. 101.
14. Letter of Shoghi Effendi, 11 March 1936, in Shoghi Effendi, *World Order*, p. 195.
15. Shoghi Effendi, *Advent*, pp. 46–7.
16. 'Abdu'l-Bahá, *Promulgation*, p. 94.
17. Bahá'u'lláh, Súriy-i-Ra'ís, *Summons*, para. 35.
18. 'Abdu'l-Bahá, *Selections*, no. 12, pp. 27–8.
19. 'Abdu'l-Bahá, *Promulgation*, p. 255.
20. ibid.
21. Bahá'u'lláh, *Hidden Words*, Arabic no. 68.

2. The Outpouring of Creative Forces

1. Bahá'u'lláh, *Tablets*, p. 141.
2. Letter of Shoghi Effendi, 25 May 1941, in Shoghi Effendi, *This Decisive Hour*, no. 82.5.
3. Bahá'u'lláh, Long Obligatory Prayer, *Prayers and Meditations*, p. 321.
4. 'Abdu'l-Bahá, *Some Answered Questions*, ch. 53.
5. 'Abdu'l-Bahá, *Promulgation*, p. 131.
6. Bahá'u'lláh, *Kitáb-i-Íqán*, p. 34.
7. 'Abdu'l-Bahá, *Selections*, p. 292.
8. Bahá'u'lláh, *Kitáb-i-Aqdas*, para. 168 and Note 155.
9. Bahá'u'lláh, *Gleanings*, p. 49.
10. ibid. pp. 76–7.
11. ibid. pp. 60–1.
12. Bahá'u'lláh, Súriy-i-Haykal, in *Summons*, para. 75.
13. Shoghi Effendi, *God Passes By*, p. 106.
14. Letter of Shoghi Effendi, 28 November 1931, in *World Order*, p. 43.
15. Shoghi Effendi, *God Passes By*, p. 237.
16. ibid. p. 58.
17. Bahá'u'lláh, *Gleanings*, pp. 92–3.
18. Shoghi Effendi, *God Passes By*, p. 110.
19. ibid.
20. ibid. p. 101.
21. Bahá'u'lláh, *Epistle*, p. 22.
22. ibid. p. 21.
23. Bahá'u'lláh, Súriy-i-Haykal, in *Summons*, paras. 6–7.
24. Shoghi Effendi, *God Passes By*, p. 107.
25. ibid. p. 152.
26. ibid. p. 244.

3. The Crystallization of Divine Forces

1. 'Abdu'l-Bahá, *Selections*, p. 20.
2. Letter of Shoghi Effendi, 8 February 1934, in Shoghi Effendi, *World Order*, p. 98.
3. Letter of Shoghi Effendi, 11 March 1936, in ibid. p. 195.
4. ibid. p. 168.
5. Letter of Shoghi Effendi, 8 February 1934, *World Order*, p. 98.
6. Letter of Shoghi Effendi, 11 March 1936, in ibid. p. 195.
7. ibid. p. 168.
8. ibid. p. 195.
9. ibid.

10. Bahá'u'lláh, quoted by Shoghi Effendi, in *Advent*, p. 31.
11. 'Abdu'l-Bahá, *Promulgation*, p. 235.
12. Letter of Shoghi Effendi, 8 February 1934, in Shoghi Effendi, *World Order*, p. 144.
13. Letter of Shoghi Effendi, 21 April 1933, in ibid. p. 89.
14. Shoghi Effendi, *God Passes By*, p. xv.
15. Letter of Shoghi Effendi, 8 February 1934, in Shoghi Effendi, *World Order*, p. 152.
16. Letter of Shoghi Effendi, 11 May 1926, in Shoghi Effendi, *Bahá'í Administration*, p. 109.
17. 'Abdu'l-Bahá, *Selections*, p. 80.
18. The Universal House of Justice, *Individual Rights and Freedoms*, para. 18.
19. Letter written on behalf of Shoghi Effendi, 20 December 1931, in *Lights of Guidance*, p. 549, no. 1864.
20. 'Abdu'l-Bahá, *Promulgation*, pp. 238–9.
21. Words attributed to 'Abdu'l-Bahá, in *Star of the West*, vol. 8, no. 8, p. 103.

4. The Progressive Release of Divine Forces

1. Bahá'u'lláh, *Tablets*, pp. 93–4.
2. Shoghi Effendi, *God Passes By*, p. 93.
3. Letter of Shoghi Effendi, 4 July 1950, in Shoghi Effendi, *Citadel of Faith*, p. 82.
4. ibid.
5. Letter of Shoghi Effendi, 15 June 1946, in Shoghi Effendi, *This Decisive Hour*, no. 158.14.
6. Shoghi Effendi, *Advent*, p. 86.
7. Letter of Shoghi Effendi, 27 November 1954, in Shoghi Effendi, *Messages to the Bahá'í World*, p. 75.
8. Letter of Shoghi Effendi, 5 June 1947, in Shoghi Effendi, *Citadel of Faith*, p. 5.
9. Letter of Shoghi Effendi, 11 March 1936, in Shoghi Effendi, *World Order*, p. 194.
10. Cable of Shoghi Effendi, 1 June 1933, in Shoghi Effendi, *This Decisive Hour*, no. 9.1.
11. Cable of Shoghi Effendi, 2 December 1946, in ibid. no. 165.1.
12. Cable of Shoghi Effendi, 26 April 1939, in ibid. no. 51.1.
13. ibid.
14. Letter of Shoghi Effendi, 4 June 1937, in ibid. no. 30.1.
15. Letter of Shoghi Effendi, February 1953, in Shoghi Effendi, *Messages to the Bahá'í World*, p. 140.

16. Letter of Shoghi Effendi, 25 October 1947, in Shoghi Effendi, *Citadel of Faith*, pp. 41–2.
17. Shoghi Effendi, *Advent*, p. 16.
18. Letter written on behalf of Shoghi Effendi, 27 March 1945, in Shoghi Effendi, *Unfolding Destiny*, p. 172.
19. Letter of Shoghi Effendi, 6 December 1928, in Shoghi Effendi, *Bahá'í Administration*, p. 154.
20. Letter of Shoghi Effendi, 25 October 1929, in ibid. p. 186.
21. ibid.
22. Letter written on behalf of Shoghi Effendi, 6 June 1948, in *Lights of Guidance*, p. 432, no. 1416.
23. Letter of Shoghi Effendi, 25 October 1929, in Shoghi Effendi, *Bahá'í Administration*, p. 186.
24. Cable of Shoghi Effendi, 25 October 1935, in Shoghi Effendi, *This Decisive Hour*, no. 18.1.
25. Letter of Shoghi Effendi, 17 June 1942, in ibid. no. 96.1.
26. Letter of Shoghi Effendi, 12 March 1943, in ibid. no.108.2.
27. Letter of the Universal House of Justice, October 1963, in the Universal House of Justice, *Messages 1963–1986*, no. 6.10.
28. Research Department of the Universal House of Justice, 'Epochs of the Formative Age', in ibid. no. 451.12b.
29. Letter of the Universal House of Justice, Riḍván 140 (1983), in the Universal House of Justice, *Wider Horizon*, pp. 5–6.
30. Letter of Shoghi Effendi, 20 November 1951, in Shoghi Effendi, *Letters to Australia and New Zealand*, p. 99.
31. Letter of Shoghi Effendi, 11 March 1936, in Shoghi Effendi, *World Order*, p. 195.

5. Universal Fermentation and the Impact of Creative Forces on Human Society

1. Bahá'u'lláh, *Gleanings*, p. 325.
2. The Báb, quoted in Shoghi Effendi, Foreword to *God Passes By*, p. xi.
3. Bahá'u'lláh, *Prayers and Meditations*, p. 295.
4. Bahá'u'lláh, *Gleanings*, p. 220.
5. Shoghi Effendi, *Advent*, p. 47.
6. Shoghi Effendi, *Promised Day is Come*, p. 3.
7. Shoghi Effendi, *God Passes By*, p. xi.
8. ibid.
9. Shoghi Effendi, *Advent*, p. 2.
10. Shoghi Effendi, *God Passes By*, pp. xi–xii.
11. Letter of Shoghi Effendi, 11 March 1936, in Shoghi Effendi, *World*

Order, p. 201.
12. Shoghi Effendi, *Promised Day is Come*, p. 122.
13. 'Abdu'l-Bahá, *Promulgation*, p. 120.
14. Shoghi Effendi, Preface, *Promised Day is Come*, p. vi.
15. ibid. p. 7.
16. Letter of Shoghi Effendi, 28 November 1931, in Shoghi Effendi, *World Order*, p. 36.
17. Shoghi Effendi (comp.), *Bahá'í Faith, 1844–1952*, pp. 42–3.
18. ibid. p. 46.
19. Letter of Shoghi Effendi, 25 May 1941, in Shoghi Effendi, *This Decisive Hour*, no. 82.1.
20. Shoghi Effendi, *Promised Day is Come*, p. 16.
21. Bahá'u'lláh, *Gleanings*, p. 213.
22. Bahá'u'lláh, Tablet to Mánik<u>ch</u>í Ṣáḥib, in *Tabernacle*, para. 1.10.
23. Bahá'u'lláh, *Kitáb-i-Aqdas*, para. 45.
24. Letter of the Universal House of Justice, October 1967, in the Universal House of Justice, *Messages 1963–1986*, no. 46.3.
25. ibid.
26. Shoghi Effendi, *Promised Day is Come*, p. 3.
27. ibid. p. 17.
28. 'Abdu'l-Bahá, in *Compilation*, vol. 1, p. 155, no. 308.
29. 'Abdu'l-Bahá, *Promulgation*, p. 429.
30. Letter written on behalf of Shoghi Effendi, 31 August 1937, in *Compilation*, vol. 1, p. 149, no. 288.
31. Letter of Shoghi Effendi, 12 August 1941, in Shoghi Effendi, *Messages to America*, pp. 51–2.
32. ibid. p. 51.
33. Letter written on behalf of Shoghi Effendi, 24 June 1936, in *Lights of Guidance*, p. 418, no. 1380.
34. 'Abdu'l-Bahá, in *Compilation*, vol. 1, p. 137, no. 268.
35. Letter of Shoghi Effendi, 20 January 1935, in Shoghi Effendi, *Dawn of a New Day*, pp. 52–3.
36. Letter of Shoghi Effendi, 18 December 1928, in *Compilation*, vol. 1, p. 175, no. 342.

6. Understanding Forces of Darkness

1. Bahá'u'lláh, *Tablets*, pp. 173–4.
2. Letter written on behalf of Shoghi Effendi, 13 March 1932, in *Compilation*, vol. 2, p. 421, no. 2251.
3. 'Abdu'l-Bahá, in *Bahá'í World Faith*, p. 384.
4. 'Abdu'l-Bahá, *Paris Talks*, pp. 60–1.
5. 'Abdu'l-Bahá, *Some Answered Questions*, p. 223.

6. Bahá'u'lláh, *Epistle*, p. 132.
7. Bahá'u'lláh, *Gleanings*, p. 149.
8. Bahá'u'lláh, *Prayers and Meditations*, p. 296.
9. 'Abdu'l-Bahá, *Some Answered Questions*, p. 264.
10. ibid. pp. 249–50.
11. 'Abdu'l-Bahá, *Paris Talks* p. 32; 'Abdu'l-Bahá, *Promulgation*, p. 10, p. 95.
12. 'Abdu'l-Bahá, *Promulgation*, p. 179.
13. ibid. p. 141.
14. ibid.
15. ibid. p. 249.
16. 'Abdu'l-Bahá, *Tablets*, vol. 3, p. 702.
17. ibid. p. 691.
18. Bahá'u'lláh, *Gleanings*, pp. 154–5.
19. 'Abdu'l-Bahá, *Promulgation*, pp. 179–80.
20. Letter of Shoghi Effendi, 21 March 1932, in Shoghi Effendi, *World Order*, p. 54.
21. The Universal House of Justice, in Bahá'u'lláh, *Kitáb-i-Aqdas*, Note 56.
22. ibid.
23. Bahá'u'lláh, *Tablets*, p. 35.
24. 'Abdu'l-Bahá, *Secret of Divine Civilization*, pp. 24–5.
25. 'Abdu'l-Bahá, in *Ḥuqúqu'lláh*, no. 23, pp. 12–14.
26. Letter of Shoghi Effendi, 11 March 1936, in Shoghi Effendi, *World Order*, p. 170.
27. Letter of Shoghi Effendi, 28 July 1954, in Shoghi Effendi, *Citadel of Faith*, p. 125.
28. 'Abdu'l-Bahá, *Promulgation*, p. 12.
29. Letter written on behalf of Shoghi Effendi, 19 July 1956, in *Lights of Guidance*, p. 131, no. 440.
30. Letter of Shoghi Effendi, 12 April 1927, in Shoghi Effendi, *Bahá'í Administration*, p. 130.
31. Letter on behalf of Shoghi Effendi, 16 April 1950, in *Lights of Guidance*, p. 78, no. 271.
32. Bahá'u'lláh, *Hidden Words*, Persian no. 40.
33. 'Abdu'l-Bahá, *Foundations*, pp. 73–4.
34. Letter of Shoghi Effendi, 12 April 1927, in Shoghi Effendi, *Bahá'í Administration*, p. 130.
35. Bahá'u'lláh, *Gleanings*, p. 65.
36. ibid. pp. 65–6.
37. Bahá'u'lláh, *Hidden Words*, Arabic no. 31.
38. Bahá'u'lláh, *Kitáb-i-Aqdas*, para. 149.
39. 'Abdu'l-Bahá, *Secret of Divine Civilization*, p. 96.

7. Combatting Forces of Darkness

1. Bahá'u'lláh, *Gleanings*, p. 200.
2. 'Abdu'l-Bahá, *Paris Talks*, p. 29.
3. 'Abdu'l-Bahá, *Selections*, p. 225.
4. Bahá'u'lláh, *Gleanings*, pp. 245–6.
5. 'Abdu'l-Bahá, *Selections*, p. 260.
6. Bahá'u'lláh, *Epistle*, p. 29.
7. ibid. p. 74.
8. Bahá'u'lláh, quoted in Shoghi Effendi, *World Order*, p. 106.
9. Bahá'u'lláh, *Epistle*, p. 55.
10. Letter written on behalf of Shoghi Effendi, 27 March 1938, in *Compilation*, vol. 2, p. 221, no. 1708.
11. Cable of Shoghi Effendi, 28 May 1953, in Shoghi Effendi, *Messages to the Bahá'í World*, p. 49.
12. Bahá'u'lláh, *Gleanings*, p. 236.
13. Shoghi Effendi, *Advent*, pp. 19–20.
14. Letter of Shoghi Effendi, 22 May 1939, in Shoghi Effendi, *This Decisive Hour*, no. 55.1.
15. Bahá'u'lláh, in *Compilation*, vol. 1, p. 368, no. 770.
16. Letter written on behalf of Shoghi Effendi, 14 May 1939, in *Compilation*, vol. 2, p. 111, no. 1468.
17. Shoghi Effendi, *Advent*, p. 59.
18. From a letter written on behalf of Shoghi Effendi to an individual, 19 April 1933.
19. Bahá'u'lláh, *Gleanings*, p. 164.
20. ibid. p. 165.
21. 'Abdu'l-Bahá, *Selections*, p. 182.
22. Letter written on behalf of Shoghi Effendi, 3 February 1937, in Shoghi Effendi, *Unfolding Destiny*, p. 436.
23. Letter written on behalf of Shoghi Effendi to an individual, 9 August 1944.
24. 'Abdu'l-Bahá, in *Bahai Scriptures*, p. 546, no. 986.

8. Custodians of the Forces of Light

1. 'Abdu'l-Bahá, *Selections*, p. 88.
2. Letter of Shoghi Effendi, 28 January 1939, in Shoghi Effendi, *Messages to America*, p. 17.
3. Shoghi Effendi, *Advent*, p. 58.
4. Letter written on behalf of Shoghi Effendi, 27 January 1945, in Shoghi Effendi, *Unfolding Destiny*, p. 442.
5. 'Abdu'l-Bahá, *Promulgation*, p. 453.
6. Letter written on behalf of Shoghi Effendi, 13 May 1945, in Shoghi

Effendi, *Letters to Australia and New Zealand*, p. 54.

7. Letter written on behalf of Shoghi Effendi, 5 February 1947, in *Lights of Guidance*, pp. 404–5, no. 1347.

8. Letter written on behalf of Shoghi Effendi, 27 March 1945, in Shoghi Effendi, *Unfolding Destiny*, p. 172.

9. Letter of Shoghi Effendi, 24 November 1924, in Shoghi Effendi, *Bahá'í Administration*, p. 68.

10. 'Abdu'l-Bahá, *Selections*, p. 140.

11. 'Abdu'l-Bahá, *Promulgation*, p. 458.

12. 'Abdu'l-Bahá, *Selections*, p. 310.

13. See, e.g. 'Abdu'l-Bahá, *Tablets of the Divine Plan*, p. 51 and Shoghi Effendi, *Bahá'í Administration*, p. 66.

14. Bahá'u'lláh, *Gleanings*, pp. 322–3.

15. Bahá'u'lláh, in *Compilation*, vol. 2, p. 293, no. 1898.

16. Bahá'u'lláh, *Kitáb-i-Íqán*, p. 173, para. 187.

17. 'Abdu'l-Bahá, *Tablets*, vol. 2, p. 244.

18. 'Abdu'l-Bahá, *Tablets of the Divine Plan*, p. 48.

19. Letter of Shoghi Effendi, 10 January 1936, in Shoghi Effendi, *Messages to America*, p. 6.

20. Letter of the Universal House of Justice, 25 May 1975, in *Lights of Guidance*, pp. 594–5, no. 2012.

21. Bahá'u'lláh, *Gleanings*, p. 335.

22. cf. 'Abdu'l-Bahá, *Makátíb-i-'Abdu'l-Bahá*, vol. 2, pp. 2–55.

23. Letter of Shoghi Effendi, 24 November 1924, in Shoghi Effendi, *Unfolding Destiny*, pp. 35–6.

24. Bahá'u'lláh, *Gleanings*, p. 320.

25. Letter of Shoghi Effendi, 21 January 1922, in Shoghi Effendi, *Bahá'í Administration*, p. 16.

26. Bahá'u'lláh, *Hidden Words*, Arabic nos. 4 and 6.

27. Bahá'u'lláh, *Gleanings*, p. 276.

28. 'Abdu'l-Bahá, *Selections*, pp. 287–8.

29. Letter of Shoghi Effendi, 11 March 1936, in Shoghi Effendi, *World Order*, p. 168.

30. 'Abdu'l-Bahá, in *Tablets*, vol. 1, p. 61.

9. **Extracts from the Writings and Messages of Shoghi Effendi on the Forces of Our Time**

1. Letter of Shoghi Effendi, 12 March 1923, in Shoghi Effendi, *Bahá'í Administration*, p. 35.

2. ibid. p. 42.

3. Letter of Shoghi Effendi, 9 April 1923, in ibid. p. 45.

4. Letter of Shoghi Effendi, 6 May 1923, in ibid. p. 49.

5. Letter of Shoghi Effendi, 14 November 1923, in ibid. p. 50.
6. ibid. p. 52.
7. From a letter of Shoghi Effendi, 30 December 1923.
8. Letter of Shoghi Effendi, 14 February 1924, in Shoghi Effendi, *Bahá'í Administration*, pp. 61–2.
9. Letter of Shoghi Effendi, 24 November 1924, in ibid. pp. 67–8.
10. ibid. p. 70.
11. From a letter of Shoghi Effendi, 26 February 1926.
12. Letter of Shoghi Effendi, 22 April 1926, in Shoghi Effendi, *Unfolding Destiny*, p. 50.
13. Letter of Shoghi Effendi, 6 December 1928, in ibid. p. 79.
14. Letter of Shoghi Effendi, 11 May 1926, in Shoghi Effendi, *Bahá'í Administration*, p. 109.
15. Letter of Shoghi Effendi, 7 October 1926, in ibid. p. 113.
16. Letter of Shoghi Effendi, 29 October 1926, in Shoghi Effendi, *Unfolding Destiny*, p. 60; and Shoghi Effendi, *Bahá'í Administration*, p. 113.
17. Letter of Shoghi Effendi, 31 October 1926, in Shoghi Effendi, *Bahá'í Administration*, p. 155.
18. Letter of Shoghi Effendi, 12 April 1927, in ibid. p. 130.
19. Letter of Shoghi Effendi, 18 October 1927, in ibid. p. 145.
20. ibid. p. 146.
21. ibid. p. 147.
22. Letter of Shoghi Effendi, 6 December 1928, in ibid. pp. 147–8.
23. ibid. p. 154.
24. Letter of Shoghi Effendi, 25 October 1929, in ibid. pp. 185–6.
25. Letter of Shoghi Effendi, 21 March 1930, *World Order*, pp. 17–18.
26. ibid. p. 19.
27. Letter written on behalf of Shoghi Effendi, 30 April 1930, in *Light of Divine Guidance*, vol. 2, p. 16.
28. Letter of Shoghi Effendi, 28 November 1931, *World Order*, p. 33.
29. ibid. p. 43.
30. ibid. p. 46.
31. ibid. p. 47.
32. Letter written on behalf of Shoghi Effendi, 20 December 1931, in *Lights of Guidance*, p. 549, no. 1864.
33. Letter written on behalf of Shoghi Effendi, 13 March 1932, in *Compilation*, vol. 2, p. 421, no. 2251.
34. Letter of Shoghi Effendi, 21 March 1932, in Shoghi Effendi, *World Order*, p. 51.
35. ibid. p. 54.
36. ibid. p. 61.
37. ibid. p. 67.

38. From a letter written on behalf of Shoghi Effendi, 29 March 1932.
39. Letter written on behalf of Shoghi Effendi, 30 March 1932, in *Light of Divine Guidance*, vol. 1, p. 41.
40. Letter of Shoghi Effendi, 27 October 1932, in Shoghi Effendi, *This Decisive Hour*, no. 5.1.
41. Shoghi Effendi, 'Epilogue', in Nabíl, *Dawn-Breakers*, pp. 667–8.
42. Letter written on behalf of Shoghi Effendi, 17 February 1933, in *Compilation*, vol. 1, pp. 84–5.
43. From a letter of Shoghi Effendi, 7 April 1933.
44. From a letter written on behalf of Shoghi Effendi to an individual, 19 April 1933.
45. Cable of Shoghi Effendi, 1 June 1933, in Shoghi Effendi, *This Decisive Hour*, no. 9.1.
46. From a letter written on behalf of Shoghi Effendi to an individual believer, 22 July 1933.
47. Letter written on behalf of Shoghi Effendi, 25 September 1933, in *Compilation*, vol. 2, p. 192, no. 1619.
48. Cable of Shoghi Effendi, 30 October 1933, in Shoghi Effendi, *Messages to America*, p. 3.
49. Letter written on behalf of Shoghi Effendi, 3 November 1933, in Ocean Research Library.
50. Letter written on behalf of Shoghi Effendi, 6 November 1933, in *Compilation*, vol. 2, pp. 192–3, no. 1620.
51. Letter of Shoghi Effendi, 8 February 1934, in Shoghi Effendi, *World Order*, p. 98.
52. ibid. p. 131.
53. Letter of Shoghi Effendi, 21 April 1933, in ibid. p. 89.
54. Letter of Shoghi Effendi, 8 February 1934, in ibid. p. 144.
55. ibid. p. 146.
56. From a letter written on behalf of Shoghi Effendi to an individual, 16 February 1934.
57. Letter written on behalf of Shoghi Effendi, 24 April 1935, in Shoghi Effendi, *Letters to Australia and New Zealand*, p. 8.
58. Cable of Shoghi Effendi, 25 October 1935, in Shoghi Effendi, *This Decisive Hour*, no. 18.1.
59. Letter written on behalf of Shoghi Effendi, 14 November 1935, in *Lights of Guidance*, p. 473, no. 1561.
60. Letter of Shoghi Effendi, 10 January 1936, in Shoghi Effendi, *This Decisive Hour*, no. 19.1.
61. Letter of Shoghi Effendi, 11 March 1936, in ibid. p. 155.
62. ibid. pp. 168–9.
63. ibid. pp. 170–1.
64. ibid. p. 188.

65. ibid. p. 191.
66. ibid. p. 195.
67. ibid.
68. ibid.
69. ibid. p. 197.
70. ibid. p. 201.
71. ibid. p. 204.
72. ibid. p. 206.
73. Letter of Shoghi Effendi, 14 November 1936, in Shoghi Effendi, *This Decisive Hour*, no. 25.1.
74. Letter written on behalf of Shoghi Effendi, 3 February 1937, in Shoghi Effendi, *Unfolding Destiny*, p. 436.
75. Letter of Shoghi Effendi, 4 June 1937, in Shoghi Effendi, *This Decisive Hour*, no. 30.1.
76. Letter written on behalf of Shoghi Effendi, 30 June 1937, in *Compilation*, vol. 2, p. 221, no. 1707.
77. Letter of Shoghi Effendi, 25 November 1937, in Shoghi Effendi, *This Decisive Hour*, no. 34.1.
78. Letter of Shoghi Effendi, 30 January 1938, in ibid. no. 36.1.
79. Letter of Shoghi Effendi, 14 April 1938, in ibid. no. 37.1.
80. From a letter written on behalf of Shoghi Effendi to an individual, 7 July 1938.
81. Letter of Shoghi Effendi, 10 September 1938, in Shoghi Effendi, *This Decisive Hour*, no. 42.1.
82. Cable of Shoghi Effendi, 22 September 1938, in ibid. no. 43.1.
83. From a letter written on behalf of Shoghi Effendi to an individual, 26 October 1938.
84. Letter written on behalf of Shoghi Effendi, 2 November 1938, in *Lights of Guidance*, p. 513, no. 1738.
85. Shoghi Effendi, *Advent*, p. 1.
86. ibid. pp. 2–2.
87. ibid. p. 16.
88. ibid. p. 18.
89. ibid.
90. ibid. pp. 19–20.
91. ibid. p. 23.
92. ibid. pp. 46–8.
93. ibid. p. 58.
94. ibid. p. 59.
95. ibid. p. 86.
96. ibid. pp. 86–7.
97. Letter of Shoghi Effendi, 8 February 1939, in Shoghi Effendi, *This Decisive Hour*, no. 47.2.

98. Cable of Shoghi Effendi, 26 April 1939, in ibid. no. 51.1.
109. ibid.
100. Letter of Shoghi Effendi, 22 May 1939, in ibid. no. 55.1.
101. ibid. no. 55.2.
102. Letter of Shoghi Effendi, 28 July 1939, in ibid. no. 58.5.
103. Letter written on behalf of Shoghi Effendi, 30 August 1939, in Compilation, vol. 2, p. 149, no. 1557.
104. From a letter written on behalf of Shoghi Effendi to an individual, 22 October 1939.
105. Letter written on behalf of Shoghi Effendi, 26 November 1939, in Lights of Guidance, p. 520, no. 1769.
106. Letter of Shoghi Effendi, 15 April 1940, in Shoghi Effendi, This Decisive Hour, nos. 70.3–4.
107. Letter of Shoghi Effendi, 15 May 1940, in ibid. no. 73.1.
108. Cable of Shoghi Effendi, 12 June 1940, in ibid. no. 74.1.
109. Shoghi Effendi, Promised Day is Come, p. 3.
110. ibid. pp. 13–14.
111. ibid. p. 95.
112. ibid. p. 104.
113. ibid. p. 118.
114. ibid. p. 122.
115. ibid. p. 125.
116. Letter written on behalf of Shoghi Effendi, 7 May 1941, in Shoghi Effendi, Dawn of a New Day, p. 199.
117. Letter of Shoghi Effendi, 25 May 1941, in Shoghi Effendi, This Decisive Hour, no. 82.5.
118. ibid. no. 82.6.
119. Cable of Shoghi Effendi, 30 June 1941, in ibid. no. 83.1.
120. Letter of Shoghi Effendi, 12 August 1941, in ibid. no. 85.5.
121. ibid. nos. 85.10–12.
122. ibid. nos. 85.13–14.
123. Letter written on behalf of Shoghi Effendi, 23 December 1941, in Lights of Guidance, p. 533, no. 1813.
124. Letter written on behalf of Shoghi Effendi, 5 April 1942, in ibid. p. 318, no. 808.
125. Letter of Shoghi Effendi, 17 June 1942, in Shoghi Effendi, This Decisive Hour, no. 96.1.
126. Letter written on behalf of Shoghi Effendi, 31 July 1942, in Compilation, vol. 2, p. 9, no. 1288.
127. Letter of Shoghi Effendi, 28 March 1943, in Shoghi Effendi, This Decisive Hour, no. 108.2.
128. From a letter written on behalf of Shoghi Effendi to an individual, 24 July 1943.

129. Shoghi Effendi, *God Passes By*, pp. xi–xii.
130. ibid. p. xii.
131. ibid. p. xiii.
132. ibid.
133. ibid. p. xv.
134. ibid. p. 58 (in reference to the Báb).
135. ibid. p. 59.
136. ibid. p. 90.
137. ibid. p. 93.
138. ibid. p. 101.
139. ibid. p. 103.
140. ibid. p. 106.
141. ibid. p. 107.
142. ibid. p. 110.
143. ibid. p. 152.
144. ibid. p. 163.
145. ibid. p. 237.
146. ibid. pp. 237–8.
147. ibid. p. 244.
148. ibid. p. 252.
149. ibid. p. 255.
150. ibid. p. 295.
151. Letter of Shoghi Effendi, 25 May 1941, in Shoghi Effendi, *This Decisive Hour*, no. 82.1.
152. Shoghi Effendi, *God Passes By*, p. 324.
153. ibid. p. 325.
154. ibid. pp. 345–6.
155. ibid. p. 354.
156. ibid. p. 355.
157. ibid. p. 379.
158. ibid. p. 402.
159. ibid. p. 405.
160. ibid.
161. ibid. pp. 411–12.
162. From a letter written on behalf of Shoghi Effendi to an individual, 9 August 1944.
163. Letter written on behalf of Shoghi Effendi, 27 January 1945, in Shoghi Effendi, *Unfolding Destiny*, p. 442.
164. Letter written on behalf of Shoghi Effendi, 27 March 1945, in ibid. p. 172.
165. Letter written on behalf of Shoghi Effendi, 13 May 1945, in Shoghi Effendi, *Letters to Australia and New Zealand*, p. 54.
166. Letter of Shoghi Effendi, 10 August 1945, in Shoghi Effendi, *This*

Decisive Hour, no. 146.6.

167. Letter written on behalf of Shoghi Effendi, 20 March 1946, in *Lights of Guidance*, p. 404, no. 1346.

168. Letter of Shoghi Effendi, 22 March 1946, in Shoghi Effendi, *Unfolding Destiny*, p. 182.

169. Letter of Shoghi Effendi, 15 June 1946, in Shoghi Effendi, *This Decisive Hour*, nos. 158.1–4.

170. ibid. no. 158.14.

171. ibid. no. 158.22.

172. ibid. no. 158.25.

173. Letter of Shoghi Effendi, 20 July 1946, in ibid. no. 160.5.

174. Cable of Shoghi Effendi, 6 October 1946, in ibid. no. 163.1.

175. Cable of Shoghi Effendi, 2 December 1946, in ibid. no. 165.1.

176. Letter written on behalf of Shoghi Effendi, 5 February 1947, in *Compilations*, vol. 2, p. 12, no. 1314.

177. Letter of Shoghi Effendi, 28 April 1947, in Shoghi Effendi, *Citadel of Faith*, p. 4.

178. Letter of Shoghi Effendi, 5 June 1947, in ibid. p. 5.

179. ibid. p. 7.

180. ibid. p. 21.

181. ibid. p. 22.

182. ibid. p. 26.

183. ibid. p. 31.

184. Letter written on behalf of Shoghi Effendi, 5 July 1947, in *Lights of Guidance*, pp. 130–1, no. 437.

185. Letter of Shoghi Effendi, 25 October 1947, in Shoghi Effendi, *Citadel of Faith*, pp. 41–2.

186. Letter of Shoghi Effendi, 25 October 1947, in ibid. p. 43.

187. Letter of Shoghi Effendi, 13 February 1948, in ibid. p. 46.

188. From a letter written on behalf of Shoghi Effendi to individuals, 20 April 1948.

189. From a letter written on behalf of Shoghi Effendi, 8 January 1949, in Shoghi Effendi, *Unfolding Destiny*, p. 454.

190. Letter of Shoghi Effendi, 18 August 1949, in Shoghi Effendi, *Citadel of Faith*, p. 77.

191. Letter of Shoghi Effendi, 22 August 1949, in Shoghi Effendi, *Letters to Australia and New Zealand*, p. 79.

192. Letter of Shoghi Effendi, 4 July 1950, in Shoghi Effendi, *Citadel of Faith*, p. 81.

193. Letter of Shoghi Effendi, 4 July 1950, in ibid. p. 82.

194. ibid. pp. 82–3.

195. Letter written on behalf of Shoghi Effendi, 4 October 1950, *Lights of Guidance*, p. 403, no. 1341.

196. Letter of Shoghi Effendi, 20 November 1951, in Shoghi Effendi, *Letters to Australia and New Zealand*, p. 99.
197. Letter of Shoghi Effendi, February 1953, in Shoghi Effendi, *Messages to the Bahá'í World*, p. 140.
198. From a letter written on behalf of Shoghi Effendi to an individual, 11 February 1952.
299. Letter of Shoghi Effendi, 4 May 1953, in Shoghi Effendi, *Messages to the Bahá'í World*, p. 153.
200. Letter of Shoghi Effendi, October 1953, in ibid. pp. 168–9.
201. Letter of Shoghi Effendi, 27 November 1954, in ibid. p. 75.
202. Letter written on behalf of Shoghi Effendi, 19 July 1956, in *Lights of Guidance*, p. 131, no. 440.
203. Letter of Shoghi Effendi, April 1957, in Shoghi Effendi, *Messages to the Bahá'í World*, p. 120.
204. Letter of Shoghi Effendi, April 1957, in ibid. p. 104.
205. Cable of Shoghi Effendi, 4 June 1957, in ibid. p. 123.
206. Letter written on behalf of Shoghi Effendi, 18 July 1957, in *Lights of Guidance*, p. 579, no. 1958.